GOSPEL-
POWERED
PARENTING

GOSPEL-POWERED PARENTING

HOW THE **GOSPEL** SHAPES AND TRANSFORMS PARENTING

WILLIAM P. FARLEY

P U B L I S H I N G
P.O. BOX 817 • PHILLIPSBURG • NEW JERSEY 08865-0817

Printed in the United States of America

Library of Congress Cataloging-in-Publication Data

Farley, William P., 1948–
  Gospel-powered parenting : how the Gospel shapes and transforms parenting / William P. Farley.
      p. cm.
  Includes bibliographical references.
  ISBN 978-1-59638-135-3 (pbk.)
  1. Parents—Religious life. 2. Parenting—Religious aspects—Christianity.
I. Title.
  BV4529.F36 2009
  248.8'45—dc22
                              2009024300

To my five children,
Sarah, Anne, Ruth, David, and Joseph

CONTENTS

ACKNOWLEDGMENTS

I want to start by thanking my parents. Through God's providential kindness, I grew up in a stable, loving home. My parents faithfully persisted in the application of their wedding vows. We just celebrated their sixtieth anniversary. For their example of dedication, love, and commitment, I will be eternally indebted. My parents disciplined me, expected big things from me, and always loved me unconditionally.

Thank you, Dad and Mom.

Second, I want to thank my beloved wife and best friend. As I will indicate many times throughout this book, parenting is a team sport. Judy is my most valued teammate. She has always supported me in front of our children, even when I did not deserve it, which was often. She has always served her husband and children lavishly. I consider her the model wife and mother. In praise I can't do better than the words of Proverbs.

> Charm is deceitful, and beauty is vain,
>> but a woman who fears the LORD is to be praised.

9

Give her of the fruit of her hands,
and let her works praise her in the gates.
(Prov. 31:30–31)

In the following pages, you will read much about the fear of God. Judy models it. For that I, our children, and our grandchildren will be eternally grateful.

In addition, she spent hours reading this manuscript back to me while supplying valuable critique. This book is the joint testimony of our parenting journey. Her fingerprints are on every paragraph.

Third, I want to thank my son Dave, who also read this manuscript and provided constructive criticism. He is a graduate of Covenant Theological Seminary and now serves as my assistant. You will read many stories about him in the following pages. You will be amazed, and encouraged, to know that he turned out so well. We serve a big God. David, thank you for your encouragement.

Also, many thanks to Dave York, pastor of Covenant Life Fellowship in Roseburg, Oregon, for his faithful reading and valuable feedback.

Many thanks to Marvin Padgett, the editor at P&R Publishing, for taking a risk with this manuscript. May it return many profits to his organization for the glory of God.

Thanks to my brothers and sisters at Grace Christian Fellowship in Spokane, Washington. They have encouraged me to write, and endured the times when I have been unavailable because of this project's demands.

Finally, and most importantly, I want to thank the living God. "For from him and through him and to him are all things"

(Rom. 11:36). This means that all that we have and are is *from* God. Any good in our lives comes by Christ's Spirit working *through* us. And in the end, our lives will be returned *to* God for his ultimate praise, honor, and glory.

This book is the fruit of God's grace working in and through an unworthy sinner. "To him be glory forever. Amen" (Rom. 11:36)!

INTRODUCTION

George Barna notes that approximately seventy-five thousand books have been published on parenting in the last ten years.[1] So why a new book on parenting? The short answer is simple: Christian parenting is in disarray. The statistics in chapter 1 will make that clear.

This is no small matter. Parenting is crucial. Success or failure can qualify or disqualify a man for spiritual leadership (1 Tim. 3:1–13). In addition, the by-product of today's parental successes or failures will determine the face and temper of the church for generations to come.

Many do not think the Bible is sufficient to equip parents. Most Christian books on parenting borrow heavily from the therapeutic world and then season the result with a few Bible verses. I wrote this book to center parenting in the Bible, more specifically the core of the Bible—the gospel. I am convinced that the gospel is sufficient to answer all our parenting questions.

Although the American family has become a polyglot of divorced spouses, homosexual couples, and unwed mothers, I have aimed this material at the increasingly rare Christian family with a female mom and a male dad, married, and living under the same roof. I hope this book will also help the millions of single parents fighting the good fight alone.

TWO EXPERIENCES

Many unique experiences have affected my approach to parenting. The first and most powerful came through reading the Bible. When my children were in their preschool years, I began to devour the Bible, especially Proverbs. When my eldest daughter was in her early teens, I discovered Reformed theology, and with it a deepening understanding of the gospel. This included a steadily expanding understanding of the *implications* of the gospel for parenting.

Second, life experience has also impacted me. For eighteen years, from my mid twenties to my mid forties, my family was in the same church. Many of our initial friends were young couples with preschool-aged children. It was a loyal, stable group of families. Our children grew up together.

We shared many experiences. We received the same teaching on how to be Christian parents. Most of it was biblical and practical. We faithfully attended church each Sunday and met in small groups throughout the week. Some of our children went to public schools, some to private Christian schools, and others were homeschooled. Our children grew up in a solid evangelical environment with all the advantages that a closely knit, cohesive Christian community can provide.

Looking back on these families and others like them, I notice the results have been mixed. Some children thrived. Their youthful faith blossomed in adulthood. They married well, and became stable, productive participants in their local churches.

Others did not fare so well. Many have completely abandoned their parents' faith. Why? What went wrong? Why did some parents succeed and others fail? Was it a failure of technique? Most of the parents disciplined their children, some more than others. We all loved them.

The results appear to have nothing to do with *where* the child was educated. In my experience, there have been no qualitative differences in the spiritual output from home schools, Christian schools, or public schools.

The common denominator between success and failure seems to be the spiritual depth and sincerity of the parents, *especially the spiritual depth and sincerity of the father.* There seems to be a strong correlation between the faith, commitment, and sincerity of the family's head and the spiritual vitality of his adult children.

My third unique experience was theological. When my eldest child was thirteen and my youngest four, I began to read *The Works of Jonathan Edwards.* To this theologian and his Puritan forebears I owe an inexpressible debt. From them I learned the centrality of the cross. In their writings I discovered the inner workings of the gospel. These lessons have dramatically shaped my parenting.

In my experience, the most effective parents have a clear grasp of the cross and its implications for daily life. The implications are manifold. They include the fear of God, a marriage that preaches the gospel to its children, deeply ingrained humility, gratitude, joy, firmness coupled with affection, and consistent teaching modeled by parents daily.

CAVEATS

All the examples in this book are about real people and real situations, but for those outside my immediate family I have changed the names and stories to preserve the anonymity of those involved. In addition, in a few cases I have combined the examples of several individuals into one story.

Throughout this book, *gospel* and *cross* are used interchangeably. Yet the cross is not the entirety of the gospel. The gospel is the incarnation of God's Son, his sinless life, his substitutionary death, his bodily resurrection, and his ascension into heaven, from which he will someday return to the earth in glory. But the cross is the heart and soul of the gospel. It is the foundation, the work, the crucial center. For this reason I sometimes refer to the cross as the gospel. The context should make the meaning clear.

Finally, this author is a sinner. My greatest sin was, and still is, unbelief—fear for my children (and now grandchildren), rather than trust in God's goodness. My second great sin, proceeding from the first, is pride, an ungodly self-confidence in my own parenting ability, a lack of dependence on God, and a failure to overflow with gratitude to God for his goodness, even when times have been tough.

Nevertheless, God has blessed Judy and me. Our married children have all married committed Christians. All serve the local church, and all of them are in a vibrant faith relationship with the Father through his Son, Jesus Christ.

I say this not to boast, but to give the reader hope. If God would do this for us, he will certainly also bless your efforts. As you read these chapters, have hope and be encouraged. God is infinitely good and gracious.

1

INTELLECTUAL
SUBMARINES

THERE I WAS, lying in bed, wide awake, my eyes searching the dark bedroom ceiling for any sign of hope.

"Are you awake?" I asked my wife, Judy.

"I can't sleep."

"Is something on your mind?" I didn't need to ask. I knew the answer. Our daughter was on a date with a friend we did not approve of. It was after midnight. In addition, since this relationship began she had been distant, obstinate, and uncooperative. Things were not well.

"I'm worried sick," my wife whispered. "I can't sleep."

I reflected on the battles of recent weeks. My once-compliant daughter had become difficult. Most distressingly, she showed little interest in Christ or spiritual things. The influence of her new friend was not good. I reflected on the title of James Dobson's book *Parenting Isn't for Cowards*. I was a coward. I needed courage. I needed hope. I had little.

"Where is she?" my wife asked. "What are they doing? She has been so different lately. I'm worried sick." Anxiety, stress, and fear dripped from her words.

I had not helped the situation. Exasperated by my daughter's sullen rebellion, I had even flirted with the idea of spanking her. My wife's commonsense appeal brought me back to reality. It was a dark time. We were discouraged and at the end of our resources. Maybe you have felt the same way.

God used this dark period in our parenting experience to deeply humble us, and we are grateful. For twenty years our parenting had been easy. We had what most would consider a model family. Sadly, we had begun to take pride in our parenting. We had begun to look down on friends with troubled teens. God's Word is clear: "Pride goes before destruction" (Prov. 16:18); "God opposes the proud" (James 4:6, quoting Prov. 3:34). We were proud. The time for humbling had come. God opposed us through our daughter's problems and brought us to our knees. We spent much time in prayer and confession. Looking back, we realize that it was a wonderful turning point.

Thankfully, our daughter also reached a turning point through this process. In a filthy Calcutta hotel (yes, India), sick with the flu and desperately homesick, this beautiful young woman finally called out to Christ. A year later God brought her a wonderful, godly husband. At this writing, they have three attractive children, and actively serve our local church. She has become a glorious gift to the church, to her husband, to her children, and to our wider family.

I told this true story to let you know that Judy and I do not "have it all together." As do all parents, we have learned from

God's gracious discipline that we are absolutely dependent on God's Spirit to complete the parenting process. We have one job—faithfulness. It is God's job to bring results!

ASSUMPTIONS

Before chapter 2 digs into this book's thesis, I want to examine some important biblical assumptions about parenting. Assumptions are the foundation for our thought life. They are unseen intellectual submarines cruising beneath the surface of our consciousness. We presume them. We seldom think about them. Yet all our conclusions about life flow from these assumptions.

In the same way, all our conclusions about *parenting* flow out of our unconscious assumptions about God, man, and ultimate reality. Collectively, they constitute our parenting worldview—a worldview diametrically opposed to that of the secular world.

Assumptions are very practical. They always put on shoes and go walking. J. Gresham Machen noted that what is today a matter of academic speculation begins tomorrow to move armies and pull down empires. Francis Schaeffer added, "People have presuppositions [assumptions], and they will live more consistently on the basis of these presuppositions than even they themselves may realize."[1] This is also true about parenting.

Your capacity to parent effectively will be a function of your assumptions. I want to discuss five assumptions that you will need in order to internalize the rest of this book.

PARENTING IS NOT EASY

Heb. 12:1

First, you cannot be a perfect parent. I opened with the story of our troubles to emphasize this point. If you could parent perfectly, your children might not need a Savior. But you are not perfect. From where you sit, you cannot even see perfection. Therefore, your children will desperately need Christ.

Your sins, failings, and inadequacies produce conflict with your children and misunderstandings with your spouse. At times you will deeply feel this inadequacy.

In addition to your inadequacies, there are external stresses. Some of your children might die prematurely, others might enter the world with congenital defects, or still others, like ours, might go through difficult stages of rebellion. Some will be bright, talented, or good-looking. Others will be slow, average, or unattractive. Some will have easy personalities. It will take all your perseverance and tenacity to love others.

Because parenting is difficult, and because you are imperfect, you will need the grace that comes to you through the gospel. God will use these problems to deepen your dependence on him. You will experience stress and obstacles. They will happen so that when your child comes to saving faith, your boasting will be in Christ, not your own best efforts. Like Paul, you will say, "I worked harder than any of them, though it was not I, but the grace of God that is with me" (1 Cor. 15:10).

You will need grace, and you will need to know where to get it. Precisely because you are so flawed, the gospel, the saving work of Christ, must be your refuge.

Effective parents don't expect a cakewalk. They assume it will be difficult but that the end result—delightful Christ-centered adult children who are married to mates that you actually like—will make it all worth the effort.

GOD IS SOVEREIGN, BUT HE USES MEANS

Second, effective parents assume two parallel truths that go off into eternity and never find a satisfactory intellectual solution. First, God is sovereign over your child's salvation: "No one knows the Father except the Son and anyone to whom the Son *chooses* to reveal him" (Matt. 11:27). This is why many from non-Christian homes become Christians. It is also why no children from Christian homes can turn to the Father unless Jesus draws them.

Second, they assume that God uses the normal means of grace to draw our children to himself. Parents are the "means" that God wants to use to reach our children. This means that we are responsible to reach our children for Christ.

Holding these two ideas—God's sovereignty and man's responsibility—in tension is important. Misunderstood, God's sovereignty can terminate in fatalism.

I knew a father whose children were completely out of control. He was passive. I was concerned, so I tentatively approached him: "I have observed your children. They seem to need discipline. They need more personal involvement and attention from you."

"God is sovereign," he answered. "He is either going to save them or not. It doesn't matter what I do. God decided their salvation in the eternal council of the Godhead before the world was created."

His response was partially true, but it was distorted by incompleteness. Yes, God is sovereign. But there is a parallel truth: *God uses means.* God gives children parents to draw them to himself. He can use other means, but he prefers parents. The point of this book is that God normally exercises his sovereignty through parents who faithfully practice biblical parenting.

We will constantly assume these two truths. God is sovereign, but parents are responsible. God's sovereignty is our hope. Parents are utterly dependent on God. He can save any child, no matter how dark the circumstances. On the other hand, God normally reaches children through their parents. It is fatal to presume upon God's sovereignty by neglecting parental faithfulness. Yet it is also a mistake to assume that it all depends on us. It doesn't. In fact, none of your efforts will prevail unless God bestows the gift of faith on your children. We are utterly dependent and responsible at the same time.

A GOOD OFFENSE

Third, effective parents assume that a good offense is better than defense.

Nothing is more deadly to a football team with a big lead than a defensive mind-set. Instead of focusing on attacking and scoring, some coaches install "prevent defenses." This strategy gives up small gains to prevent the "big play." The mentality of the team members shifts from scoring themselves to preventing their opponent from scoring. We have all watched this approach forfeit huge leads to an opponent with an aggressive, offensive, attacking mentality.

Parents can do the same thing. Dr. Tim Kimmel calls it "fear based parenting."[2] Either we can focus on preparing our children to enter the world and conquer it, or we can concentrate on protecting our children from the world. A defensive mind-set worries about the evil influences of Halloween, Santa Claus, the Easter Bunny, or non-Christians on the Little League team. Although parenting always involves some protection, this should not be the main focus for biblical parents.

Often this defensive mentality is the fruit of legalism. The legalistic parent usually assumes that his or her children are born again. But this parent has little confidence in the *power* of new birth. Therefore, parenting is all about protecting the children from evil outside influence.

This approach can be deadly. A friend who graduated from a solid evangelical high school, and was still in contact with members of his graduating class, recently informed me that most of them (over 70 percent) smoke pot and engage in sexual promiscuity. "What went wrong?" I asked.

"Because they went to church and attended a Christian high school, their parents assumed their children were born again," my friend answered.

Since these parents presumed their children's new birth, all that remained was protecting them. That is why many of them sent their children to Christian high school.

Another example is a pastor friend who has five grown children. Only one is following Christ today. What went wrong? A man who knew him well described his parenting this way: No

TV, no movies, no public education, no non-Christian friends. In other words, his focus was defensive, protecting his children.

This book will assume that effective parents have an offensive mind-set. It will assume that your children are not Christians. It will assume that they need the overwhelming, all-conquering power of new birth. It will assume that, once they get it, its power will protect them from the world. "He who is in you is greater than he who is in the world" (1 John 4:4). First John 5:4 reads, "Everyone who has been born of God overcomes the world." And according to 1 John 3:9, "No one born of God makes a practice of sinning, for God's seed abides in him, and he cannot keep on sinning because he has been born of God."

In other words, this book will assume that effective parents equip their children to overcome the world—not by changing and controlling their environment (things external to their children), but by going after *their children's hearts.* We change their hearts by teaching the gospel, modeling the gospel, and centering our homes on the gospel. The gospel, rightly understood and modeled, makes Christianity attractive. Effective parents make the gospel so attractive that the world cannot get a foothold in their children's hearts.

Thomas Chalmers (1780–1847), a Scotch Presbyterian, wrote a famous essay entitled *The Expulsive Power of a New Affection.* In it Chalmers proposes that the best way to overcome the world is not with morality or self-discipline. Christians overcome the world by seeing the beauty and excellence of Christ. They overcome the world by seeing something more attractive than the world: Christ, "in whom are hidden all the treasures of wisdom and knowledge" (Col. 2:3). A man who owns an Acura is not interested in a Geo Metro. In the same way, Christian parents try to make Christ and his kingdom glorious. Their children conquer the lusts of this world with a higher passion: the moral beauty of Christ.

By contrast, defensive parents have little confidence in the attractiveness of the gospel. They think the world is more powerful. Fundamentally, they are not confident in the gospel's power to transform their children from the inside out. They do not believe Jesus' words, "Take heart; I have overcome the world" (John 16:33). They have little confidence in the world-conquering power of new birth.

My wife and I have seen the fruit of this approach in our own experience. My five children all attended public high schools, and then the eldest four matriculated to a state university. Despite the raunchy non-Christian—even anti-Christian—environment (and it was foul), they thrived spiritually. Why? Through the miracle of new birth, God changed their hearts. To them the Holy Spirit had begun to unveil the superlative value of Jesus Christ. The conviction that all their happiness was tied up in their relationship with Christ had begun to bud and grow. The world's allurements could not compete.

When they arrived at college, they immediately sought out Christian fellowship. We didn't make them do this. We didn't even suggest it. They did it because their hearts were already in God's kingdom. They thrived in this environment. They found and married vibrant Christian mates.

How did we give this to our children? We didn't. We couldn't. This change only God can give. It was the miracle of new birth. I am and will be eternally grateful for his *unmerited* grace and mercy toward Judy and me. Here is my point:

Our parenting approach was fundamentally offensive, not defensive. We aimed all our arrows at our children's hearts, knowing that once their hearts had been changed, the decisive battle was fought and won. The rest of their lives would be just mop-up.

By contrast, many parents who assume their children's new birth have little confidence in the new birth they assume, and therefore pour their energies into protection. Many times their children never actually receive new birth. They leave home, grateful to be away from their parents' rules and regulations. They have no heart tools to fight off the world's allurements. They go where their hearts want to go, to the party scene far from God.

What motivates the defensive approach? I am convinced that parents with a defensive mind-set usually fail to understand the power of the gospel. They have little confidence in the power of new birth. They don't understand the role of the heart in conversion and sanctification. Instead, they emphasize the child's external environment. They put their confidence in rules, restrictions, and protections.

UNDERSTAND NEW BIRTH

Fourth, effective parents understand new birth. Statistically, most Christian parents assume their child's new birth. This could be your biggest parenting mistake.

WORLD magazine cites a new book by Christian Smith and Melinda Lundquist Denton, *Soul Searching: The Religious and Spiritual Lives of American Teenagers.*[3] After surveying three thousand American teens about their religious beliefs, the authors summed them up with the phrase *Moralistic Therapeutic Deism*, or *MTD*.

These teens believe in a combination of works-righteousness, religion as psychological well-being, and a distant, noninterfering god.[4] Ironically, many of these young deists are active in their churches. "Most religious teenagers either do not really comprehend what their own religious traditions say they are supposed to believe," conclude Smith and Denton, "or they do understand it and simply do not care to believe it." The article's author goes on to note that "MTD has become the 'dominant civil religion.' And it is 'colonizing' American Christianity. . . ."[5]

It is important for every Christian parent to discern MTD from Christianity. A child can be compliant and well-behaved, attend Sunday worship, and socialize with the church youth group, but merely possess MTD. Many "nice" people are not Christians. Being "nice" has little to do with Christianity.

The sexual habits of evangelical children also reveal the prevalence of MTD. Sociologist Mark Regnerus in his book *Forbidden Fruit: Sex & Religion in the Lives of American Teenagers*[6] exposes the failure of evangelical homes to discern and mold their children's spiritual values.[7] The author points out that evangelical teenagers are just as sexually active as their non-Christian friends. In fact, there is evidence that evangelical teenagers on the whole may be *more sexually active.* Those who identify themselves as evangelical teens tend to have their first sexual encounter at a younger age, 16.3 years, than liberal Protestants, who tend to lose their virginity at 16.7 years. And young evangelicals are far more likely to have had three or more sexual partners (13.7 percent) than non-evangelicals (8.9 percent). What about abstinence pledges? Those work—for a while—delaying sex on an average by about eighteen months, with 88 percent of pledgers eventually giving up their vow.

These and similar findings suggest that American evangelical teens are substantially no different from their unbelieving friends. Why? I want to suggest that one crucial assumption explains these dismal statistics.

Most Christian parents assume that church attendance or youth-group involvement equates to new birth. Parents are naive about new birth and its symptoms. "One key reason that evangelicals often don't stand out," notes Regnerus, "is [that] the measure itself—affiliating with an evangelical Protestant congregation—is not a measure of dynamic religiosity but simply one *of affiliation*. . . . There is no shortage of religiously apathetic evangelical adolescents and adults in America."[8]

Regnerus makes a good point. "Affiliating" with a church is not Christianity. As the old saying goes, your child can sleep in the garage for a month, but that won't make him a car. Your children must be born again to "see" or "enter" God's kingdom (John 3:3–5).

Even a child's testimony that he "accepted Jesus" or "asked Jesus into his heart" means very little. That is because God initiates new birth. Of course, the child is responsible to respond to God with faith and repentance. But a child can go through these steps and not have the saving faith and repentance that point to new birth. That is why it is foolish for parents to presume upon new birth. New birth is a radical change of heart that ushers in new desires, new loves, and a new life direction.

"No one born of God makes a practice of sinning, for God's seed abides in him, and he cannot keep on sinning because he has been born of God" (1 John 3:9). It means that the child now owns Christianity for himself.

Tom Bisset notes four reasons why evangelical teens abandon the faith in droves. The fourth is that they failed to own it for themselves.[9] In other words, they were never born again. A. W. Pink observes that

> The new birth is very much more than simply shedding a few tears due to a temporary remorse over sin. It is far more than changing our course of life, the leaving off of bad habits and the substituting of good ones. It is something different from the mere cherishing and practicing of noble ideals. It goes infinitely deeper than coming forward to take some popular evangelist by the hand, signing a pledge-card, or "joining the church." The new birth is no mere turning over a new leaf, but is the inception and reception of a new life. It is no mere reformation but a complete transformation. In short, the new birth is a miracle, the result of the supernatural operation of God. It is radical, revolutionary, lasting.[10]

I recently asked a panel of four young married couples when they came to Christ. They all said something like this: "I asked Jesus into my heart when I was at grade school summer camp, but I didn't really get serious about Christianity until I was in my late teens or early twenties."

I responded, "So what you are really saying is, 'I asked Jesus into my heart when I was in grade school, but my life didn't really revolve around Jesus, he was not really on the throne of my life, I did not increasingly trust him with my life and future, until I was a young adult.' Is that right?"

"Yes, that is a good description."

"New birth," I responded, "means that one has enthroned Christ in the center of one's life. You become a Christian when your life, thinking, and behavior begin to revolve around Jesus Christ. Until that happens, professions and decisions mean little. Changed behavior proceeding from a spiritual heart transplant is the only certain evidence of new birth."

My friends were like so many of us. They had simplistic ideas about new birth. They thought a decision for Christ was the same thing as new birth. But the truth is different. Conversion is outside of our control. God is sovereign over the process. "The Son gives life to whom he will" (John 5:21). In his book *Spiritual Birthline*, Stephen Smallman writes, "The lesson learned from the birthline—that we cannot cause spiritual birth, nor can we make the birth happen until it is ready—applies to our children as well. We trust God, but we are also willing to wait."[11]

The bottom line is this: New birth is known by its fruits, not by a decision. The most important fruit is hunger for God himself. Effective parents assume this, and patiently wait for sustained fruit before they render a verdict.

God *gives* new birth to the children of parents who please him. Neither the child nor the parent can earn new birth. It is a gift of grace. But those who believe, and live as though they really believe, please him. One expression of the faith that pleases God in parents is the fear of God. (More on this in chapter 3.)

He is sovereign. Sometimes he regenerates children of parents who do not please him. Sometimes new birth is sudden and dramatic. The recipient remembers the day and hour. And sometimes the Christian is not sure when it occurred. For most, it occurs during a process of growing into faith. The person cannot identify the exact moment or day.

New birth normally comes to children through the teaching, example, and relationship that they have with their parents, especially the father. Parents are God's means of grace given to effect the child's conversion.

The moral is simple: Be wise. Don't presume your child's new birth until you see solid evidence. The first sign is growing hunger for God. Other signs are hunger for holiness, growing obedience to parents, and desire for secret prayer and Bible reading.

CHILD-CENTERED FAMILIES

Fifth, effective parents are not child centered. They are God centered. They strive to put God at the center of their family. The eighteenth-century New England Puritan pastors warned their congregations not to love their children too much. If they lived today, they might say, "Don't put your children at the center of your life. That spot belongs to God."

Ken and Jackie were sincere parents. But their sincerity was their problem. They loved their children. In fact, they loved them too much. The oldest son was a talented athlete. He excelled on the local U16 soccer team. Because the team practiced during the dinner hour, the family stopped eating meals together. They had been in the habit of praying and reading the Bible after meals. This also ended.

Their daughter was an exceptionally talented ballerina. Her lessons were expensive. Ken and Jackie couldn't afford them and tithe at the same time. *We will resume tithing when she graduates*, they rationalized.

Fig. 1. Child-Centered Family

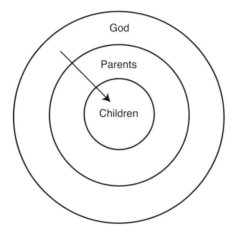

Soon the family was traveling to weekend soccer tournaments. Most were on Sunday, so church attendance became increasingly sporadic. Slowly, their social world began to revolve around the other soccer parents rather than their church family. Although their son and daughter attended the church youth functions, soccer and ballet always came first. At age sixteen, their daughter began to audition with professional ballet troupes in distant cities. Soon the family was traveling to her weekend auditions.

Eventually the children went off to college. Within a few years they had both quit attending church. They forgot God. They threw themselves into their real interests, athletics and dancing. Ken and Jackie were deeply troubled. *What went wrong? What can we do to get our children back?*

Fig. 2. God-Centered Family

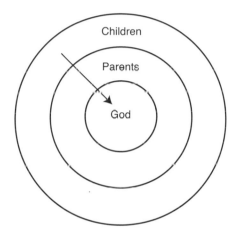

They had made a common mistake. They centered their family around their children. It is important to love your children, but there is a fine line between healthy parental love and child worship. We know the latter has happened when we begin compromising God's will for the sake of our children or their activities. Ken and Jackie stopped tithing and praying together as a family. They made soccer and ballet, not the local church, the center around which their family orbited. (See Figure 1.) Compromise always points to idolatry. It displeases God. He does not like competitors, especially when they are our children.

Ken and Jackie's children imitated their parents. Mom and Dad taught them well. Church was not important. God was not at the center of their lives. What really mattered were their children's activities. Ken and Jackie had placed their children, and their success, on the throne of the family. Their children heard the message, understood it, and imitated it.

By contrast, Tim and Angie centered their home in God and his will (Figure 2). Tim told his son's soccer coach, "My son will be available any day but Sunday. I'm sorry if this inconveniences the team, but God is more important to us than soccer." This was a problem. Tim's son was the best player on the team. They needed him to win. The coach and the other players put tremendous pressure on Tim to compromise, but he refused to budge.

In the same way, when Tim found out that his daughter's piano lessons would be during their family dinner hour, he gently asked her to find another teacher, reminding her that the family dinner hour was sacred. It was the only time for the family to be together, and that family unity was more important than her piano lessons.

Tim's decisions might seem small, but they had immense long-term consequences. Tim centered his family in God and his will. Ken centered his family in his children. God was at the center of Tim and Angie's family. Ken's world orbited around his children. Tim's decisions disappointed his children in the short run, but won them for Christ in the long run. Ken and Jackie thought they were loving their children, but they were actually forfeiting their children's respect, driving them away with overindulgence.

Paul's first letter to the Corinthians describes what a God-centered family looks like: "But I want you to understand that the head of every man is Christ, the head of a wife is her husband, and the head of Christ is God" (1 Cor. 11:3). For Paul, the Christian family is hierarchical. *Hierarchy* is a nasty word in our anti-authoritarian culture. Yet heaven, a world of intense joy, love, and peace, is profoundly hierarchical. God the Father is Lord of all, God the Son submits to his authority, and the Holy Spirit delights to obey both Father and Son.

To the degree that heaven permeates our homes, they also will be hierarchical. Christ is the Head of every husband. He rules by dying. The husband is the head of his wife. God asks him to rule the same way. Children submit to God through their parents.

In a God-centered family, everyone serves God by submitting to the authority over them. The husband focuses on pleasing God, not his wife. The wife focuses on pleasing God by submitting to her husband's authority rather than pleasing her children. The children please God by honoring and obeying their parents.

This concept applies equally to single parents. The head of the family might be a single mom, but she is still the head of her family, and she can still bring her home under God's gracious rule.

Where a family centers itself—God or children—will first depend on where the family's head centers himself. Is he seeking to please God or his children? Is he willing to disappoint his family to please God, or does he fear their disapproval? Does he have a clear grasp of God's will for his family, or have the nuances of the therapeutic age effectively evangelized him?

Does he fear God's disapproval, or does he fear his family's disapproval?

A God-centered family also requires the cooperation of a godly mate. Can she trust God to speak through her husband, or does she resist his efforts to lead? Is she willing to trust God to parent her children through her husband, or is she constantly grasping for the reins of power and control? Does she encourage her man to lead, or does she fear his leadership?

The symptoms of God-centeredness are numerous. The first is a willingness to say "no" to a child when it is in the child's best interest. A second symptom is a marriage in which Dad and Mom are united before their children, even when they disagree about a parenting direction. A third symptom of God-centeredness is the willingness to make our marriages more important than our children. Our children are with us for only eighteen to twenty-five short years. Most marriages have as many years without children as they do with. It is a big mistake to put your children ahead of your marriage. A fourth symptom is a willingness to be different. God-centered homes will be radically different.

In conclusion, it is positively hurtful to build your lives around your children instead of God. It damages children, it tears down our marriages, and most importantly, it displeases God.

SUMMARY

This chapter argues that assumptions are important. Ultimately, they put on shoes and go walking, practically affecting our parenting. We briefly looked at five assumptions that parents need to make. First, effective Christian parents assume that parenting will not be easy, but that the rewards will ultimately make it all worthwhile.

Second, effective Christian parents are willing to hold God's sovereignty and their responsibility in tension.

Third, effective Christian parents assume an offensive mind-set. They pursue their children's hearts. They do everything possible to make the gospel attractive. Protecting their children from worldly influence is not their fundamental goal.

Fourth, effective Christian parents are shrewd about new birth. They do not assume it. They understand the nature of new birth, and they carefully look for its symptoms.

Fifth, effective Christian parents labor to focus their families on God, not their children.

In all of this, we have continually referenced the gospel. The thesis of this book is that the gospel empowers effective parenting. To that argument we now turn in chapter 2.

STUDY QUESTIONS

1. In a few words, how would you sum up the main point of this chapter?

2. With what assumptions did your parents raise you? How have their assumptions affected your approach to parenting?

3. Which assumption in this chapter is most important to you at your current stage of parenting?

4. Which assumptions mentioned in this chapter have you not assumed? Why?

5. Can you think of any other assumptions that would be important to a Christian parent's worldview?

6. Which of these assumptions are most difficult to live out? Why?

7. What pressures from our culture make these assumptions difficult to believe and apply? Why?

2

GOSPEL-POWERED PARENTING

HAVE YOU EVER overlooked something obvious?

One day the electric heat in our home stopped working. It was winter. It was icy cold, and I was desperate. I took the thermostat down, tore it apart, and checked for defects. Nothing! I checked all the wiring in the house. Everything seemed to be working. After thirty minutes of frantic searching and testing, I finally gave up and called the heating technician. It was a Saturday morning.

"Since it is the weekend, the repairman's rate is one hundred dollars per hour," the office secretary kindly warned. "We start the clock when he leaves the shop, and it stops when he returns."

I swallowed hard. What could I do? The family was cold. We couldn't wait until Monday.

"Thanks for the warning," I said. "But I am desperate. Send him out!"

About an hour later the repairman appeared at the door with an assortment of impressive tools dangling from his belt. Flashlight in hand, he disappeared into our basement. Five minutes later he returned.

"I have good news," he grinned. "It was a simple fix. The breaker to the electric heat was in the 'off' position. I flipped it back." He handed me a bill for $150.

To say that I felt foolish would be an understatement. What could be more *obvious* than the breaker? And yet, it was the one place I hadn't thought to look.

Spiritual things work the same way. Sometimes we overlook the obvious. Concerning the task of parenting, the most overlooked, obvious source for help is the gospel. We assume it, but rarely see its application to child raising. Yet it is as fundamental to effective parenting as the breaker is to our electric heat.

Paul tells us that the gospel "is the power of God for salvation" (Rom. 1:16). But its power does not end there. The gospel is also the power of God for parenting. We argued in the first chapter that our children's hearts are the issue. Effective application of the gospel empowers parents to reach their children's hearts.

That is the thesis of this book. But before we develop it, I want to pause and define *parenting*.

PARENTING DEFINED

There are many definitions of *parenting*. For example, Wikipedia notes that "parenting is the process of raising and educating a child from birth until adulthood."[1] For Christians, however, this definition is inadequate. It ignores the ultimate goal of parenting—eternity.

Christians parent with one eye on eternity. Their children will live *forever*. This is a staggering thought. We cannot imagine "forever." Nevertheless, the destiny of our children either will be love that surpasses knowledge, joy inexpressible and full of glory, coupled with peace that passes understanding, or it will be weeping, wailing, and gnashing of teeth. There is no middle ground. Therefore, the Christian does not parent for this life only. The believing parent labors to prepare each child for the day of judgment. The stakes are inexpressibly high.

To borrow a metaphor from Randy Alcorn, if the duration of a child's life were a line that stretched forever, the child's time on earth would be a tiny period at the beginning of that line that would be almost invisible to the naked eye. That would still be the case if the child lived for ten thousand years because any finite time period, set next to eternity, becomes increasingly small as the line of eternity gets longer and longer. Your child will not live for ten thousand years. His or her life expectancy is about seventy-five to eighty years. More significantly, our one chance to influence that destiny lasts for only about *eighteen* short years.[2] We get one shot. There are no second chances.

Christian parents have one goal during this short window of opportunity. It is to transfer the baton of faith in Christ to the next generation. Victory does not always go to the fastest four-hundred-meter relay team. It goes to the team that most efficiently transfers the baton. No matter how fast the runners, if the transfer is slow and clumsy, that team will probably lose. In the same way, parents prepare their children for the day of judgment by transferring their faith, values, purposes, self-discipline, and motivations to their children.

Therefore, we can summarize Christian parenting this way: Parenting is the process of transferring our worldview to the next generation. By *worldview* I mean the beliefs, values, self-discipline, and purposes just mentioned.

NOT MORALITY

It is important to note that the primary focus of Christian parenting is not morality. Well-behaved children are not the ultimate end. Saving faith, deeply rooted in the children's hearts, is the supreme goal of Christian parents. God saves the child who transfers all his trust from his own works to Christ's and expresses that faith with repentance. Therefore, Christian parenting is all about the transfer of Dad and Mom's faith. Morality is important, but it follows faith. It does not produce it.

In fact, *moralism*—the idea that we merit God's favor by being good—is the deadly enemy of Christian parenting. Moralism trusts in its own goodness, virtue, and principled intentions to get a "not guilty" verdict from God on the day of judgment. It is deceptive. A cloak of morality over an unregenerate heart can make it difficult to discern the child's true spiritual condition. Paul rejects moralism: "We hold that one is justified by faith apart from works of the law" (Rom. 3:28). And in Galatians he adds, "We know that a person is not justified by works of the law but through faith in Jesus Christ" (Gal. 2:16). Moralism inculcates an ugly self-reliance that is the enemy of true Christian parenting. On the day of judgment God will condemn it.

Transferring morality is the primary goal of secular parenting. For unbelievers, the goal of parenting is children that conform to society's expectations, such as admittance to Ivy League schools, success in business, or marriage to the "right" people.

By contrast, the goal of Christian parenting is heart transformation. As we have noted, morality always follows that transformation, but it is secondary. This means that effective Christian parents aim at their children's hearts rather than their behavior. In *Shepherding a Child's Heart*, Tedd Tripp notes, "A change in behavior that does not proceed from the heart is not commendable, it is condemnable."[5]

Mom asked Johnny to sit in the corner. With a sullen look he obeyed but said, "I'm sitting down on the outside, but on the inside I'm still standing up." This is not heart transformation. It is moralism. It is the attitude of many teens from Christian homes: "I'm a Christian because my parents are, but I would really rather be at the party." It describes many adult Christians: "I go to church because I was raised that way, but my real passion is golf, hunting, or _____ [fill in the blank]." This is not the fruit of successful Christian parenting.

In summary, Christian parenting is the process of preparing our children for the day of judgment. We do that by transferring our worldview to them. Our worldview is the sum of our beliefs, values, purposes, and self-control. Parenting has not succeeded until God's worldview has conquered a child's heart.

WHERE ARE THE SCRIPTURES?

We expect the Bible to speak most frequently at the point of our greatest need. Where the shoe leather of daily life meets the road of daily experience, we anticipate and need biblical instruction. For example, money is an important part of daily life. The Bible contains hundreds of Scriptures on money. Relationships are also a big part of our life. The Bible does not disappoint us. There are hundreds of verses describing to whom and how we should relate.

In the same way, parenting is a major concern for most adults. From the first child's birth until the last child leaves home, twenty-five to thirty years for most couples, parenting occupies us twenty-four/seven. Since the future of our children and grandchildren rides on our success or failure, we want and need biblical instruction.

But to our great disappointment, when we go to the Bible for direct instruction, mostly bare cupboards stare back. The New Testament contains only two verses on this important subject: "Fathers, do not provoke your children to anger, but bring them up in the discipline and instruction of the Lord" (Eph. 6:4); "Fathers, do not provoke your children, lest they become discouraged" (Col. 3:21).

Each text is short and to the point. And to our consternation, they make the same point—don't provoke your children to anger. Paul does not even define what it means to provoke them to anger.

The Old Testament helps a little, but not as much as we would like. Most of the direct instruction on parenting is in two chapters of Deuteronomy and a few passages from Proverbs.

Why so little direction? The biblically uninformed might conclude that God doesn't care about our children or that parenting is unimportant. The truth is exactly the opposite. God is even more passionate about our children than we are.

The good news is that God wants your children in his kingdom. Most parents assume that God loves their children. The day will come, however, if it hasn't already, when you are going to need God's assurance that he is "with" your children. The prophet Isaiah gave Israel that assurance.

> "And as for me, this is my covenant with them," says the LORD: "My Spirit that is upon you, and my words that I have put in your mouth, shall not depart out of your mouth, or out of the mouth of your offspring, or out of the mouth of your children's offspring," says the LORD, "from this time forth and forevermore." (Isa. 59:21)

And in the middle of a passage against divorce, the prophet Malachi says,

> And what was the one God seeking? Godly offspring. So guard yourselves in your spirit, and let none of you be faithless to the wife of your youth. (Mal. 2:15)

Maybe the Holy Spirit forgot to address parenting when he put the canon of Scripture together. No, the God who has numbered every hair on our heads has made no mistakes about the content of Scripture.

Instead, the scarcity of parenting texts is deliberate, premeditated, and precise. God knows there are only two in the New Testament; this is no mistake.

Why so few? The answer is so simple and probably so obvious (like my failure to check the breaker when my furnace went down) that it is easy to miss. There are so few Scriptures because *the gospel is the classroom that teaches us everything we need to know to become effective Christian parents.* If we really understand the gospel, and know how to apply it to our marriages and parenting, we have all the tools we need to pass the baton to our children.

SEVEN WAYS IN WHICH THE GOSPEL AFFECTS PARENTS

The gospel makes parents effective in seven ways.

1. The gospel teaches Christian parents to fear God. Parents need this crucial virtue. More than any other quality, God promises to bless the parents who fear him. Chapter 3 will argue this point from Scripture. Chapters 4 and 5 will explain why and how the gospel motivates Christian parents to fear God.

2. The gospel motivates parents to lead by example. Paul tells us in Ephesians 5 that God created the institution of marriage to proclaim the gospel. Our children are the first audience impacted. God wants our children to see our marriages, behold the beauty of the gospel, and be irresistibly attracted.

The gospel makes parents increasingly (but never perfectly) humble, consistent, and affectionate. These qualities probably do more to transfer a parent's faith, self-discipline, motivation, and values to his children than anything else. How this takes place is the subject of chapter 6.

46

3. The gospel centers families in their male servant leaders. Christianity is a patriarchal religion. In both the local congregation and the home, men lead. Gospel-centered churches attract men. Gospel-centered churches encourage men to become servant leaders for their wives and children. Gospel-centered churches encourage biblical masculinity. You can be a male and not be masculine. How the gospel builds men is the subject of chapter 7.

4. The gospel teaches and motivates parents to discipline their children. It displays the horror of sin. It illustrates its consequences. Therefore, gospel-centered parents persevere in the discipline of their children. The gospel also teaches parents *how* to discipline their children. In addition, teaching the gospel becomes the end of all Christian discipline. How the gospel affects discipline is the subject of chapters 8 and 9.

5. The gospel motivates parents to teach their children. The primary teachers of children are not schoolteachers or Sunday-school teachers, but their parents. The gospel is also the essential content of their teaching. How the gospel motivates and shapes what we teach our children is the subject of chapter 10.

6. The gospel motivates parents to lavish their children with love and affection. We make the mistake of assuming that all parents love their children. Most parents feel affection for their children, but few love their children with Christ's love. The gospel motivates parents, especially fathers, to love children sacrificially, as Christ loves his church. The gospel defines what Christ's love looks like. How the gospel does this is the subject of chapter 11.

7. *The gospel is the solution for inadequate parents.* Parents often feel the weight of their failures and inadequacies. No matter how hard they try, their parenting is always woefully inadequate. The gospel is the solution, described in chapter 12. Gospel-centered parents run to the cross every day for mercy, forgiveness, and hope to reapply themselves to the task of parental fidelity.

GOSPEL DEFINED

Since the gospel is going to be our paradigm for parenting, we need to pause and define it. Our English word *gospel* translates the Greek word *evangelion*, which simply means "good news" or "glad tidings." But "good news" or "glad tidings" have no context apart from bad news. The gospel is wonderful news only to those who know they are in trouble. We are sinners. Sin alienates us from God. Even worse, it makes us God's enemies. It exposes us to God's eternal judgment.

This is the bottom line for everyone. There are no exceptions. The testimony of Scripture is clear: "Enter not into judgment with your servant, for *no one living is righteous* before you" (Ps. 143:2). "As it is written: '*None is righteous, no, not one*'" (Rom. 3:10). And "I know that nothing good dwells in me, that is, in my flesh. For I have the desire to do what is right, but not the ability to carry it out" (Rom. 7:18).

God is infinitely just. His justice compels him to judge sin impartially and without exception. God's justice distributes both punishment and reward. Wrath is what perfect justice insists that sin deserves. God's wrath appears in different ways in our experience. In the end it is the ultimate cause of most human suffering. Because of God's wrath, we are born sinners. Because of sin, we get sick and die. Because of sin, women deliver babies in excruciating pain. Because of sin, over fifty million people died in World War II. Because of sin, babies are born deformed, marriages end in divorce, and people commit suicide. Our temporal suffering, however, is just the tip of the iceberg. After death, if one's sin has not been forgiven, a hell of eternal suffering awaits each sinner. As Cornelius Plantinga reminds us, "things are not the way they are supposed to be."[4] We live in a fallen world. Without the black backdrop of our sinful nature and its consequences (God's wrath), the gospel is a big yawn. Yet we are indeed in trouble, and the gospel is the solution.

To those who believe the bad news, the gospel is the most wonderful news that anyone could hear. God so loved the world that he sent his Son to save us from the bad news. The gospel is the good news that the Son of God humbled himself, vacated his throne of glory, descended an *infinite* distance, and became a slave first to his Father and then to fallen men. Finally, he submitted to death by slow torture on a Roman cross (Phil. 2:5–8). Why? Love impelled him. He died in our place. He took the judgment that we deserve. "God so loved the world, that he gave his only Son, that whoever believes in him should not perish but have eternal life" (John 3:16). As R. C. Sproul so eloquently puts it, Christ came to save us from his own wrath. Put another way, Christ came to save us from himself.[5]

On the third day, he rose from the dead. Forty days later, he ascended into heaven and sat down at his Father's right hand. The Father gave him the Holy Spirit, which he poured out on Pentecost. He continues to pour it out today. The Holy Spirit comes to impress our hearts with the reality of these wonderful truths. The Holy Spirit is gospel-centered.

This is the good news. The gospel clothes us in Christ's righteousness. It initiates us into the experience of the Father's amazing love. It removes God's wrath and alienation. It does all of this at God's infinite personal expense and without causing him to compromise the perfections of his glory.

The cross is the heart of the gospel—in John Piper's words, its blazing center. The cross is the ethic of the gospel. It models the behavior that God wants his people to imitate. As Augustine noted, the cross is God's pulpit. From it he proclaims the gospel. From it the Father preaches his love (Eph. 3:19). On the third day the Father raised his Son to vindicate the work accomplished on the cross. He sends the Holy Spirit to make all of this real to fallen, sinful men.

In the final analysis, all these gospel truths culminate in the cross. Wise parents go there for direction, wisdom, and counsel.

INEFFECTIVE ALTERNATIVES

Parents can substitute many things for the gospel. Contemporary books such as *The Ten Basic Principles of Good Parenting, Playful Parenting, How to Talk So Kids Will Listen,* and *The Price of Privilege* contain some useful information. But they speak from a non-Christian worldview. They assume radically different answers to life's big questions: What is life's purpose and destiny? What is the nature of authority? What does appropriate discipline look like? What is human nature like? What happens after death?

Others replace the gospel with therapy. Trends such as "Attachment Parenting" and "Positive Parenting," as well as others, compete for our attention. Many Christian books on parenting draw more assumptions from modern therapy than the clear assumptions about God and man that underlie the gospel. But none of these affect children like the simplicity of the gospel.

Still others replace the gospel with religion. "If I just take them to church or get them into a youth ministry, they will be okay." But religion and its trappings are no substitute for the gospel.

The emphasis of this book differs from that of many other Christian books on parenting. Most emphasize techniques. By contrast, *Gospel-Powered Parenting* will emphasize the parents' relationship with God, with each other, and with their children, in that order. The emphasis of this book is that parenting is not primarily about doing the right things. It is about having a right relationship with God—a relationship informed by the gospel.

SUMMARY

Christian parenting is the process of preparing our children for the day of judgment. We do that by transferring our worldview to them. There is little direct biblical instruction on parenting because the gospel is the tutorial that informs our parenting. The gospel is the good news that Jesus died to save us from a terrible fate. The gospel focuses on, and centers in, the cross of Christ. Although secular alternatives may have some value, the gospel is the power of God for parenting. Gospel-centered parents get gospel-powered results.

STUDY QUESTIONS

1. What was the main point of this chapter?

2. After reading this chapter, how would you define *parenting*?

3. The author stated that moralism is the deadly enemy of parenting. What is moralism? Why did the author say this? Do you agree or disagree?

4. Why are there so few Scriptures on how to parent?

5. This chapter discusses seven ways in which the gospel impacts parenting. Which one surprised you the most? Why? Which two of these seven do you think are most important?

6. Describe any ways that your parenting has been influenced by "ineffective alternatives" common to our culture. How do these methods need to change in order to conform to a biblical worldview?

3

GOSPEL FEAR

NEW BIRTH is the ultimate change that every child needs. It is the goal of the parenting process.

I have five children. Two received new birth before they were old enough to remember. Three received new birth in their teens or later. One of these received new birth at age sixteen. The change was immediate and decisive. Before new birth he was moral, participated in our church youth group, and attended church. He and his friends considered him a Christian, but his heart was not in it. After new birth he began to pray in secret and read his Bible. He displayed a new interest in obeying his parents. He began to seek out Christian friends. In short, he was no longer a Christian just because his parents were. He owned the faith for himself. When this happened, the war was over. We had fought and won the decisive battle. From this point forward, our parenting was primarily mop-up. The change of heart that comes with new birth solves many lesser parenting problems.

But every parent faces a dilemma. We cannot give our children new birth. Children cannot take it. They cannot purchase it. We cannot earn it. "But to all who did receive him, who believed in his name, he gave the right to become children of God, who were born, not of blood nor of the will of the flesh nor of the will of man, but of God" (John 1:12–13).

God gives new birth, and he gives it to whomever he wills. "No one knows the Father except the Son and anyone to whom the Son *chooses* to reveal him" (Matt. 11:27). Therefore, as we saw in chapter 1, every parent is profoundly dependent on God to finish the parenting process by giving each child new birth.

Since this is true, the most important thing that parents can do for their children is to learn how to please God. We please God by faith. But there is a specific expression of saving faith that attracts God's favor to parents. It is the heart and soul of parental effectiveness, and it is the last virtue that most would expect.

Business writers who can isolate the few activities responsible for corporate success make a lot of money. That is because those activities are difficult to define, isolate, and practice. Peter Drucker's classic, *The Effective Executive*, attempts to do that. He attempts to identify the qualities that most effective executives share in common. *In Search of Excellence* by Thomas Peters and Robert Waterman does the same for corporations. What are the essential values and practices that consistently make corporations successful?

In the same way, the Bible consistently isolates a core expression of faith and attributes parental success to it. It is a fruit of the gospel. The Bible calls it the *fear of God*. The biblical promises to parents who possess it are profound and numerous. In fact, it is the most important thing that parents can possess to move God to regenerate their children. In short, God blesses the children and grandchildren of the parents who learn and practice the fear of God. This may sound like moralism—God blessing us because we are good. It is not. God blesses faith, and a key expression of faith is the fear of God.

I need to pause here for a disclaimer. This book presents general principles that usually get results. But God makes no absolute guarantees to parents, such as: *If you do _____ [fill in the blank], all your children will become Christians.* God is sovereign. He determines how and when each child enters his kingdom. Yet God repeatedly tells us that he delights to bless certain principles. A minority of the children of the Christian parents who do not practice these principles will follow Christ. On the other hand, the majority of the children of the Christian parents who practice them will enter Christ's kingdom.

A PERSONAL STORY

Several years ago my wife and I met a gifted minister from Australia. I will call him John. He possessed unusual abilities, and God had given him tremendous responsibilities. He oversaw about a hundred churches in the Philippines. He supervised churches in New Zealand as well as many in the western United States. Even churches in British Columbia looked to him for leadership. He had great political influence in Australia and pastored a large church there.

We always looked forward to his visits. He spoke at our summer camps. His preaching energized and expanded our spiritual vision. He seemed to be on the cutting edge of God's activities.

This man had written several popular books and booklets. His ministry published a monthly magazine with an international circulation. He constantly traveled, lecturing at conferences and churches around the Pacific Rim. God gave John great privileges, and John seemed capable and called to these responsibilities.

One day the shocking news arrived that a relative had confronted John about secret sexual immorality. We were stunned. At first, we refused to believe the rumors. John was a spiritual George Washington. He seemed to radiate integrity. Reluctantly we eventually learned the ugly truth. John's outward appearance and his inward life were a contradiction. The sordid details of his sin eventually confirmed our worst fears.

For many years John had kept up a series of adulterous liaisons in the cities where he habitually traveled. He managed to hide this from everyone except the only One who counts: the omniscient, ever-seeing God who judges the universe. This God eventually exposed John's darkness in his holy, white Light.

A few days after his sin was exposed, the doctors found a tumor behind John's right eye. Within a few weeks he was dead. His lack of repentance was the most frightening aspect of this story. A pastor friend visited John at his bedside, hoping to lead him to repentance. He begged John to confess and repent of his sexual immorality, but John would not.

John's true story demonstrates both the incredible compassion *and* the awesome justice of the living God. We know that he is amazingly patient with us. He is "slow to anger" (Ex. 34:6). It came out later that John had persisted in this sin for at least ten years. God could have exposed it at any time, but he gave his servant every opportunity to repent. When God's patience finally ran out, however, his judgment was swift and painful. "Note then the kindness and severity of God: severity toward those who have fallen, but God's kindness to you, provided you continue in his kindness" (Rom. 11:22).

Many would assume that John's tumor was just a coincidence: "Certainly it was not the judgment of God!" Yet I sincerely believe it was exactly that. Paul's sobering words addressed to the Ephesian Christians support my conviction: "Let no one deceive you with empty words, for because of these things [sexual immorality, in this case] the *wrath of God* comes upon the sons of disobedience" (Eph. 5:6). Because God is compassionate, gracious, and slow to anger, the consequences for sin do not always immediately follow. There are always consequences, but they are not always immediate.

John made the same fatal mistake that many others make. He mistook God's *patience* with sinners for the idea that God is *tolerant* of sin. After six or seven years of immorality, John must have reasoned, "There has been no judgment. God must not care. I must be a special exception to God's normal rules." But it is always a grave mistake to presume upon the mercies of God.

SCRIPTURES

Because it is so easy to distort, the concept of the fear of God is often ignored by the church. But the Bible claims that it is the key to friendship with God (Ps. 25:14), the fruit of single-mindedness (Ps. 86:11), the secret to wealth, riches, and long life (Prov. 10:27; 22:4), and the key to the wisdom that builds families (Prov 9:10; 24:3). In short, the fear of God is a fountain of life (Prov. 14:27) that quenches the thirst of those who possess it.

God makes lavish promises to the parents who learn to fear him. For example, when Abraham was an old man, God commanded him to sacrifice his son Isaac. As Abraham lifted his knife over his beloved boy, the angel of the Lord stopped him: "Do not lay your hand on the boy or do anything to him, for now I know that you *fear God*, seeing you have not withheld your son, your only son, from me" (Gen. 22:12).

Abraham's fear pleased God. It appeared in action. It expressed saving faith. Notice the connection between Abraham's fear and God's willingness to bless his posterity.

> By myself I have sworn, declares the LORD, because you have done this [have feared me] and have not withheld your son, your only son, I will surely bless you, and I will surely multiply your *offspring* as the stars of heaven and as the sand that is on the seashore. And your *offspring* shall possess the gate of his enemies, and in your *offspring* shall all the nations of the earth be blessed, because you have obeyed my voice. (Gen. 22:16–18)

Abraham obeyed God. His obedience was a by-product of great faith. The angel referred to that faith as "fear[ing] God." Because of it God blessed Abraham's descendants. Many have argued that Abraham's family has been the most influential in history. Every Christian is a child of Abraham. His legacy, which continues to this day, demonstrates the direct connection between the fear of God and blessed posterity.

A second example of this principle occurred several hundred years later. Looking back on Israel's golden-calf idolatry at Mount Sinai, God lamented to Moses, "Oh that they [Israel] had such a mind as this always, to fear me and to keep all my commandments, that it might go well with them and *with their descendants* forever!" (Deut. 5:29).

These words reveal God's anguish. He wanted to bless the people of Israel and their descendants. The condition was fearing him. But Israel would not fear him, and therefore he would not be able to bless their children forever.

Psalm 25:12–13 continues this theme: "Who is the man who fears the LORD? Him will he instruct in the way that he should choose. His soul shall abide in well-being, and his *offspring* shall inherit the land." Notice again the connection between the parent's fear of God and blessed descendants.

Psalm 103:17 continues this theme: "But the steadfast love of the LORD is from everlasting to everlasting on those who fear him, and his righteousness to *children's children*." God's righteousness, both imputed and practical, and his great love surround the descendants of the parent who fears God.

How about Psalm 112:1–2? "Blessed is the man who fears the LORD, who greatly delights in his commandments! His offspring will be mighty in the land; the generation of the upright will be blessed."

Psalm 128:1–4 reads: "Blessed is everyone who fears the LORD, who walks in his ways! You shall eat the fruit of the labor of your hands; you shall be blessed, and it shall be well with you. Your wife will be like a fruitful vine within your house; your children will be like olive shoots around your table. Behold, thus shall the man be blessed who fears the LORD."

If you think this is an Old Testament concept, consider Mary's prayer in Luke 1:50: "And his mercy is for those who fear him from generation to generation."

The verses do not end here. There are more! The conclusion? Those who believe these promises, and love their children, will want to grow in the fear of the Lord.

Those who think the fear of the Lord is an Old Testament concept believe that when Jesus unveiled God's love at the cross, the fear of God died. After all, doesn't 1 John 4:18 read that "perfect love casts out fear"?

Perfect love does cast out fear, but it is the fear of everything *except* the fear of God. No, the fear of God is a New Testament concept. The fear of God so prominent in the Old Testament actually culminates in the gospel. The cross reveals the reason to fear God more clearly and accurately than everything in the Old Testament combined. Before we prove this, let us pause to define the fear of God.

FEAR OF GOD DEFINED

Often people ask why they should fear God. Many object, "God saves us by grace through faith alone. Paul tells us that the Holy Spirit cries 'Abba, Father' from within all true saints. How does the fear of God mesh with these truths?" The biblical answer is simple, and John's heartbreaking story, like many biblical examples, illustrates it. *We fear God because sin always has consequences.* We must understand that we can be under the weight of these consequences and still be saved.

In our desire to keep people from needless guilt and insecurity, we often shy away from this truth, yet God has salted the pages of the Bible with numerous confirming verses and stories. It is not our job to comfort the weak by manipulating God's Word or by teaching it selectively. We must compassionately present God's entire counsel. In his timing God will comfort the weak, convict them, and teach them to delight in the fear of God.

Chapter 2 defined *parenting*. We stated that one reason there are so few Scriptures on parenting is that the gospel contains all we need to know to become effective parents. We showed that successful parents practice the fear of God. We suggested that we learn the fear of God in the New Testament, at the cross. In other words, we learn it from the gospel. We learned that parents are dependent on God to initiate their child's salvation, and that God is most likely to give new birth to the child whose parents practice the fear of God.

Therefore, a clear understanding of the fear of God is important. One obstacle to understanding the fear of God is the struggle to synthesize the fear of God and the love of God. How can I experience the love of God and fear him at the same time? This question really presents a false dichotomy. The two are not opposed. Rather, they are mutually dependent. You cannot separate the fear of God from the experience of his love. God's perfect love amplifies the fear of God, and the fear of God intensifies his love. It is impossible to fully know and experience God's love without learning to fear him. Again, the two are not mutually exclusive. They are joined at the hip.

Although many have attempted it, in my experience, *the fear of God* is difficult to define. It is an oversimplification to say that this fear does not involve dread. God told Isaiah that he should "dread" God (Isa. 8:13). And the New Testament adds, "It is a fearful thing to fall into the hands of the living God" (Heb. 10:31). "The fear of the Lord," writes Ed Welch, "like the fear of people, involves a spectrum of attitudes. On one side the fear of the Lord does mean a terror of God."[1]

But it is an opposite error to assume that this fear minimizes a deep and abiding peace and security in God's presence. The blood of the Lamb that makes us righteous should daily prompt parents who fear God to cry, "Abba, Father!" (Rom. 8:15). Welch continues, "Knowing the difference between these two fears clarifies why Scripture can say 'There is no fear in love' (1 John 4:18) while simultaneously demanding the fear of God."[2]

The believer's fear of God is not the slavish fear found in the Old Testament. Rather, it is grounded in a sense of God's holiness, his hatred of evil, the judgment my sin deserves, and the horrible fate of unbelief. Mingled with all of this is a profound sense of sonship, adoption, God's free grace, and his extravagant, glorious, unearnable love. Those who rightly fear God increasingly revel in his infinite grace. The more one fears God, the more he or she confesses with Paul that nothing "will be able to separate us from the love of God in Christ Jesus our Lord" (Rom. 8:39).

The fear of God has two expressions. One helps us; the other hinders us. One attracts us to God; the other repels us from God. Moses' experience at Mount Sinai illustrates the difference. There God appeared to Israel in blazing fire concealed by thick clouds. It was terrible. The ground trembled. Lightning pierced the sky. Heavenly trumpets blasted. His voice shook the earth. "When the people saw the thunder and the flashes of lightning and the sound of the trumpet and the mountain smoking, the people *were afraid and trembled*, and they stood far off and said to Moses, 'You speak to us, and we will listen; but do not let God speak to us, lest we die'" (Ex. 20:18–19). The people were afraid—and rightly so. It was a frightening sight. But note Moses' important and curious response: "*Do not fear*, for God has come to test you, *that the fear of him may be before you*, that you may not sin" (Ex. 20:20).

Moses' answer sounds paradoxical. First he tells the Israelites, "Do not fear." Then he tells them that God has come to teach them the fear of God. Was this Old Testament double-talk, or was Moses trying to say something important? Within this paradox lies the key to understanding the fear of God. What Moses really meant was, "*Do not fear God in the wrong way, as slaves.* God has come to test you and cause you to *fear him in the right way, as sons.* Those who fear him as sons obey God and keep his commandments."

Slave-dread, the wrong type of fear, does not motivate obedience. It causes us to run away from God. Notice that the Israelites "stood far off." Those with slave-dread draw back from God. They have no conviction that he is good, that he rewards those who seek him, or that he has their best interests at heart. All they see is his holiness, his severity, and his hatred of sin, and they run the other way. By contrast, son-fear motivates us to pursue God. Although the people drew back, Moses went right up the mountain into the fiery cloud to be near God.

I live within two hours of Grand Coulee Dam, a huge concrete structure spanning the Columbia River in central Washington State. Grand Coulee is the largest and most spectacular Columbia River dam. Although I had heard much about the sheer size and majesty of this dam, only in its presence could I comprehend its immensity. Standing below the dam, arching my neck to see its top towering three hundred feet above me, thinking about the 150-mile lake straining and pushing in an attempt to collapse its confining bulk, and watching small rivulets of water leaking from its cold concrete face, I began to tremble. I felt small, helpless, vulnerable, and easily destroyed. *If the dam fails, I will be instantly crushed in a torrent of unstoppable water.* It was one thing to read about this engineering marvel; it was something completely different to stand in its presence. I couldn't wait to get into the car and get away from the base of that dam. That is what slave-dread is like. It causes us to run away from God.

But son-fear, the fear that comes with new birth, attracts us to God. It motivates us to pursue God. As we have seen, the people of Israel drew back from Mount Sinai, but Moses went right up the mountain into the fiery cloud to be near God. Why? Like Israel, Moses saw the holiness of God. He saw what his sin deserved. But he also saw the goodness of God. He saw that the Lord is compassionate and gracious, slow to anger, abounding in steadfast love and mercy (Ex. 34:6), and that he does not give us what our sins deserve (Ps. 103:10), but removes our transgressions from his presence as far as east is from west (Ps. 103:12). Moses' fear was more like the fear that attracts us to the edge of the Grand Canyon. We are afraid, but the incredible beauty and vastness of the great gulf irresistibly compels us. It puts life in context, and gives us great peace.

Here is another difference: People with slave-fear do not obey God, but son-fear motivates obedience. That is why Paul tells us that the fear of God completes holiness (2 Cor. 7:1). It motivates us to work out our salvation with fear and trembling (Phil. 2:12). To fear God as a son is to hope in his steadfast love (Ps. 147:11). It equips us to exult, "His steadfast love endures forever" (Ps. 118:4). God bestows his steadfast love on those who fear him (Ps. 103:11, 17). His compassion pursues those who fear him (Ps. 103:13).

The Son of God is the most important proof that son-fear has these effects. No one pursued God like Jesus. No one experienced the Father's love like Jesus. And yet, no man has ever perfected the fear of God like Jesus. Speaking of the Messiah, the prophet Isaiah predicted that "the Spirit of the LORD shall rest upon him, the Spirit of wisdom and understanding, the Spirit of counsel and might, the Spirit of knowledge and the *fear of the LORD*. And his delight shall be in the *fear of the LORD*" (Isa. 11:2–3). Jesus delighted in the fear of the Lord. So does every Christian who discovers it. They delight in it. Their children and grandchildren delight in it.

Which fear do you think of when you think of "the fear of the Lord"? Many think of slave-dread. They can't figure out why the Bible promises so many benefits to the man who possesses it. To them, it is entirely negative. It should be—it is the fear of unbelievers.

By contrast, son-fear is wholly positive, but it is little discussed in the modern church. Maybe that is why so few of our children follow God. A life saturated in it perfects holiness and exposes us to God's incomprehensible love. It is son-fear that makes parents powerful and effective.

Fearing our heavenly Father is something like fearing a good earthly father. I feared my father. I knew that he would inflict whatever pain was necessary to instill in me obedience, loyalty, hard work, and perseverance, among other things. But I also hoped in his love. I felt secure in his presence. I knew that he would not reject me—that no matter what I did, he would never stop loving me. I could disappoint him. I could grieve him. But I could not motivate him to withdraw his love from me. Many reading this paragraph did not have a father like this. Whether you did or you didn't, this is what God's love is like. This is what fearing God is like.

I said that all the Old Testament verses about the fear of God culminate in the gospel. The cross of Christ is the greatest reason to fear God in the Bible. At the foot of the cross we learn son-fear, the fear that motivates God to bless our children. At the cross of Christ we obtain the skills needed to pass the baton to the next generation. In the next chapter we will begin to explore how and why this is true.

WHAT TO EXPECT

This book will continually return to the fear of God. The fear of God teaches parents to fear God, not their children. It motivates parents to discipline their children. It attracts men to family and church. It inspires parents to discipline their children in a wholesome, upbuilding way. It motivates parents to be compassionate and affectionate. It rivets our eyes on eternal realities, the shortness of this life, and the immensity of eternity for which our parenting is our child's crucial preparation. It makes parents humble, teachable, and approachable. In short, the fear of God is the beginning of wisdom (Prov. 9:10), and the wisdom that this fear teaches us is the crucial building material for our homes. "By wisdom a house is built, and by understanding it is established" (Prov. 24:3).

SUMMARY

Your children need new birth, but you do not have power to give it to them. God saves; parents do not!

Throughout Scripture, however, God makes lavish promises to the parents who learn to fear him. More than any other virtue, the fear of God attracts God's favor to our parenting. The fear of God is difficult to define. There is a carnal fear that drives one away from God. There is a wholesome, spiritual fear that attracts the believer to God. It knows that God is holy, but it also has a deep conviction that he loves us and is on our side. The latter is the fear that God blesses.

Some think the fear of God is an Old Testament concept, one that expired with the coming of the New Testament. Yet nothing could be further from the truth. The fear of God actually finds its culmination, and purest expression, in the New Testament, at the cross of Christ. Psalm 130:4 reads, "With you there is forgiveness, that you may be feared." God has designed forgiveness, received through our redemption, to provoke the fear of God. This is why gospel-centered parents are so effective. They learn the fear of God at the foot of the cross. This fear attracts us to the Father and also perfects holiness in us and our children (2 Cor. 7:1).

In the next two chapters we will discover why Psalm 130 connects the fear of God with the knowledge of our forgiveness.

STUDY QUESTIONS

1. In your own words, describe what this chapter was about.

2. Before you read this chapter, what did *fear of God* mean to you?

3. How did this chapter change your understanding of the concept of the fear of God?

4. In your opinion, why is the fear of God so important to parenting?

5. How do you think that having the fear of God would change the way in which parents related to their children?

6. What was your favorite paragraph in this chapter? Why?

7. What can a parent do to grow in the fear of God?

4

A HOLY FATHER

THE PREVIOUS CHAPTER argued that God blesses the parenting of those who learn to fear him. It concluded with the statement that we best learn the fear of God not in the Old Testament, but from the gospel in the New Testament. This chapter and the next will explain why this is true.

Have you ever noticed that most books on parenting—Christian and secular—emphasize technique? "This is how you should do it. Follow these four steps and you will be successful."

This book will take another approach. I want to change your thinking, especially how you think about God and yourself. If I am successful, the techniques will take care of themselves. That is because what we do is a by-product of how we think. People change their behavior as their understanding of God and man changes.

But this presents a problem. Publishers tell us that many Christian parents will not expend the mental sweat necessary to think deeply about God and man. In other words, today's parent avoids the *T*-word—*theology*. I trust that you won't do this. It is a significant roadblock to parenting—even though it is the American way of life.

We are as we think. We parent out of our theology. Everyone, Christian and non-Christian, has a theology—an idea of who God is and who we are by contrast. Some are accurate. Some are not.

Theology is the study of God. Theological emphasis is unique to Christianity. That is because Christians don't earn salvation. It is a gift. Rodney Stark notes that the other world religions all share one teaching in common: self-salvation. Therefore, their focus is on behavior rather than God. They study rules and regulations—how to be good, to meet God's standard. But because Christians believe that salvation is God's gift, which can't be earned, they study the giver. They focus on right belief about God himself—that is, theology.[2]

The next two chapters are the heart and soul of this book. They are about the theology of God. That is where parenting must start. If you understand chapters 4 and 5, and if you really see God with the eyes of your heart, my job will be mostly done, and this book will probably succeed in its aim, even if you don't read the following chapters that apply this theology.

GOSPEL FUNDAMENTALS

I played basketball for my high school team. The coach stressed fundamentals—layups from the right and left side, passing, defense, and rebounding. After many hours on these drills, we often became frustrated. "Coach, we want to practice dunking. Let's have a contest to see which player can do the most spectacular dunk." (We had only two players who could dunk, but we all loved to try, and we loved to watch the two that could.)

Predictably, the coach would answer. "Dunking doesn't win games. Fundamentals win games. I know they're boring; they're not spectacular. I know they don't make the crowd stand up and cheer. But the team that is best at the fundamentals wins the game." He was right. We were not very talented, but we were good at the fundamentals. We went 18 and 2 that year.

That was my junior year. The next year we got a new coach. He did not stress fundamentals. Against the same teams (and players) we went 2 and 18. I learned an important lesson: Fundamentals win games.

Christian parenting works the same way. The cross is the fundamental of Christianity. It is also the deepest and most profound Christian truth. In the world of parenting, the fundamentals get results. You can understand this principle superficially, or you can understand it profoundly, but how you understand it will shape your parenting.

I just watched the DVD series *Planet Earth*. One of the segments is devoted to caves. It opens with a man diving into the entrance of a vertical cave. The cave doesn't look deep until the man disappears with his parachute still unopened. (He didn't die. He eventually opened his chute.)

The gospel is like this cave. From the surface, it might appear shallow. But the more we understand it, the further we fall without opening our chute. Its depths swallow us up as we continue to fall.

This chapter is a short primer on what the cross tells us about the Father's holiness, his separateness, and his wrath toward sin. Don't get discouraged. The next chapter will explore God's grace. Work your way through it, slowly if you need to. For the sake of your children and grandchildren, grow in the knowledge of God the Father.

GOD IS HOLY

The cross convinces us that our heavenly Father is infinitely holy.

Let's make a word association. What comes to mind when you think of the word *holiness?* To some it connotes smells and bells: incense, liturgy, stained glass, and high-ceilinged stone cathedrals. To others it means solemnity, long faces, always being good, and missing out on all the fun.

This is not biblical holiness. "Holiness means *separation,*" writes Philip Ryken. "Something holy is *set apart.* In the case of God, holiness means that he is set apart from everything he has made. Holiness is not simply his righteousness (although that is part of it), but also his *otherness.* It is the *distinction* between the Creator and the creature, the *infinite* distance between God's divinity and our humanity."[3]

Here is another way to say it: The more holy someone or something is, the more separate he or it is from things that are common or normal. The opposite of holiness is not sinfulness. It is commonness—or, to use the old word, profaneness.[4] When God says he is holy, he means that he is different from us. He means that he constantly and actively separates himself from all sin, wickedness, evil, and moral corruption—that is, all that is common to this world.

My wife is allergic to the fragrance of some flowers. They make her eyes red and sore. When that happens, we separate her from the flowers. We put the flowers on the back porch. This is the idea behind holiness. It is as if God were allergic to evil in all its forms, and he must immediately remove himself.

Morally, this means that God is distinct and unique from everything with which we are familiar. He is not what we expect. We would never invent the God of the Bible. Invented gods are like the people that invent them. They are not separate. They are common. That is because we make them in our own image.

God is holy. That means that he is perfect, pure, and spotless in a way that we cannot imagine. Everything about God is holy. "You . . . are of purer eyes than to see evil and cannot look at wrong" (Hab. 1:13). "The heavens are not pure in his sight" (Job 15:15). "Who will not fear [you], O Lord, . . for you *alone* are holy" (Rev. 15:4). His throne is holy (Ps. 47:8), his name is holy (Ps. 30:4), and his arm is holy (Ps. 98:1). As A. W. Tozer has noted, "Neither this writer nor the reader of these words is qualified to appreciate the holiness of God. We know nothing like the divine holiness. It stands apart, unique, unapproachable, incomprehensible, and unattainable. The natural man is blind to it."[5]

Holiness is God's fundamental attribute. It is the most important thing to know about him. It is where we start with God. His holiness defines all his other attributes. We fear his wrath because it is holy, and we admire his love precisely because it is holy. Day and night, those closest to him, the cherubim and seraphim, cry: "Holy, holy, holy is the LORD of hosts" (Isa. 6:3). Everything about God is holy. The Bible calls him the "Holy One" fifty-eight times. His Spirit is a *Holy* Spirit. Therefore, Scripture commands us to "worship the LORD in the splendor of holiness" (Ps. 29:2).

Throughout redemptive history, God has constantly separated himself from sin and sinners. When Adam and Eve sinned, God "drove out the man, and at the east of the garden of Eden he placed the cherubim and a flaming sword that turned every way to guard the way to the tree of life" (Gen. 3:24).

When the iniquity of the Jews reached its climax, God deported them from Jerusalem, the place where his presence dwelt, to Babylon. He separated them from himself. God's manifest presence also departed from the temple (Ezek. 10).

Eventually God will even separate himself from creation. The world is not the way it is supposed to be. Sin has corrupted it. Job reminds us that "even the moon is not bright, and the stars are not pure in his eyes" (Job 25:5). This is why, on the day of judgment, we find God separating himself from fallen creation in order to form a new universe undefiled by sin: "Then I saw a great white throne and him who was seated on it. From his presence earth and sky fled away, and no place was found for them" (Rev. 20:11).

Ultimately, God will separate himself forever from everyone not reconciled to him by faith in his Son: "Then he will say to those on his left, '*Depart from me*, you cursed, into the eternal fire prepared for the devil and his angels' " (Matt. 25:41).

Everything the Bible says about the holiness—the separateness—of God the Father is summed up in and emphasized by the cross. The cross is an exclamation point at the end of God's holiness.

HOLINESS UNVEILED

The cross was the most graphic demonstration of the Father's holiness in human history. To understand it, we need to reflect on the Father's love for his Son.

The Father's love for his Son is intense: "This is my beloved Son, with whom I am well pleased" (Matt. 3:17). It is not a common love. It is holy. He loves his Son with omnipotence, which means all power, with infinite intensity. He also loves his Son with omniscience—all knowledge. His gaze penetrates the infinite perfection of his Son's deity. Since the Son's glory is infinite, only an infinite intellect can fully know and love him. He knows the Son exhaustively, and what the Father knows and sees is the infinite perfection of the Son's divinity.

But here is the stunning truth: Such is the holiness of the Father that when his Son bore our sin and transgressions, *God separated himself from him.* "My God, my God," Jesus cried from the cross, "why have you forsaken me?" (Matt. 27:46). What can we say in the face of this staggering truth? How can we imagine such holiness? As A. W. Tozer notes,

> We cannot grasp the true meaning of the divine holiness by thinking of someone or something very pure and then raising the concept to the highest degree we are capable of. God's holiness is not simply the best we know infinitely bettered. We know nothing like the divine holiness. . . . [We] may fear God's power and admire His wisdom, but His holiness we cannot even imagine. Only the Spirit of the Holy One can impart to the human spirit the knowledge of the holy.[6]

The cross convinces us of this truth. God is holy. He always separates himself from sin and sinners. This insight is crucial to parenting. *Effective parents increasingly see sin through God's eyes.* They increasingly feel it with God's feelings. They are clear on the issues. If God hates sin so much that he would separate himself even from his only Son when he bore our sin, how much more will he separate himself from our children if they are not reconciled to him through the miracle of new birth?

But the other side is also true. If God so loves both us and our children that he willingly forsook his only begotten Son in order to reach us, we have great confidence. If we do our job as parents, God will be faithful to us and our children. We also have great obligation. How great will be the accounting to a God who loves our children this intensely. How will we answer him if we neglect our duty?

HOLY WAYS REVEALED

Holiness also means that God's ways are different from our ways. "As the heavens are higher than the earth, so are my *ways* higher than your *ways* and my thoughts than your thoughts" (Isa. 55:9). The cross makes the separateness (holiness) of God's ways clear.

"What was the ultimate cause that led to Christ's coming to earth and dying for our sins?" asks Wayne Grudem. He answers, "The love and justice of God."[7] Love we understand, but justice? The common way to handle an offense is to let bygones be bygones, to forgive and forget. But God is holy. His ways are not our ways. He is just, and his justice is holy. It is not like this world's justice. It cannot be suspended, compromised, or ignored. It must be executed with perfection. It must be satisfied. In other words, it would be sin for God to compromise justice.

Because God is holy, he cannot forgive without punishing sin. The cross gave God a way to both forgive and satisfy divine justice at the same time. When God forgives a guilty sinner, it is only because his justice has been satisfied. God has punished it in his Son at the cross.

Here is how it happened. God put the sins of all believers, Old and New Testament, on his Son. Then he punished those sins with the torments they deserve. In this way, God is able to forgive the offender without compromising his holy justice. The cross equips God, simultaneously, to be both "just and the justifier of the one who has faith in Jesus" (Rom. 3:26).

The cross reminds us that God is holy. His ways are not our ways. His thoughts are not our thoughts (Isa. 55:8). In the same way, the "ways" of effective Christian parents are holy. They are different from the world around them. We will return to this topic later.

HOLY WRATH

God is not someone we invent or make up. He is objective. He has told us (in the pages of Scripture) what he is like. Therefore, it serves us to pay close attention. I have said this because our next subject, God's wrath, is difficult. It is a subject that you will be tempted to ignore or suppress. What the gospel tells us about it is not pleasant.

As we have seen, God's holiness provokes him to *hate* evil and passionately love all that is good, virtuous, and true. This is a problem for the modern mind. *Hate* has become a four-letter word. The media denounces "hate speech." In fact, for many, anyone with strong convictions is guilty of "hate."

But the Bible consistently describes God's hatred, and for him it is always virtuous. He never apologizes for it. He doesn't feel guilty about it. "You [God] hate all evildoers" (Ps. 5:5). "You [God] have loved righteousness and hated wickedness. Therefore God, your God, has anointed you [the Messiah] with the oil of gladness" (Ps. 45:7). "I have loved Jacob but Esau I have hated" (Mal. 1:2–3).

Wrath is the form taken by this "hatred" of evil. It is holy wrath. When infinite goodness and evil collide, wrath is the overflow. "God's wrath arises from His intense, settled hatred of all sin," observes Jerry Bridges. It "is the tangible expression of His inflexible determination to punish it. We might say God's wrath is His justice in action, rendering to everyone his just due, which because of our sin, is always judgment."[9]

Most of us are reluctant to face up to the wrath of God. That "God is love" (1 John 4:16) we are all sure. But wrath? How can I worship a God who gets angry? Isn't anger a sin?

But the Bible discusses the wrath of God more frequently than his love. "In the Old Testament more than twenty words are used of the wrath of God," notes Leon Morris. "The total number of references to God's wrath exceeds 580, so that it cannot be said to be an occasional topic. In the Bible the wrath of God is intensely personal."[10] I think A. W. Pink was right: "Our readiness or our reluctance to meditate upon the wrath of God becomes a sure test of how our hearts really stand affected towards [God]."[11]

Human wrath is usually sinful. Human wrath is anger out of control. It is unrighteous. But God's wrath is never out of control. Rather, it is measured. It is deliberate. Most importantly, God is "*slow to anger*, and abounding in steadfast love and faithfulness" (Ex. 34:6).

This means that God's anger is tightly controlled. It is more like the anger of the Ents in J. R. R. Tolkien's fantasy *The Lord of the Rings*. In Tolkien's story, the Ents are powerful living trees that grow in Middle-earth. For generations they sleep. They finally awake to a Middle-earth dominated by evil. Their anger grows, but very slowly. They do nothing hastily. But when it finally erupts, their collective wrath wreaks devastation on the evil city nearby. This is a good picture of how God's wrath works. God's wrath is never sinful. Rather, it is an expression of his holiness. It is one of God's moral perfections. It is an important aspect of his glory.

The real question is not: "How can God be loving and wrathful at the same time?" Rather, the real question is: "How could God be good—infinitely good in the way the Bible describes him—and *not* feel intense anger at sin and evil?" Sin destroys everything it touches. It destroys the glory of God. It distorts individual happiness. It corrupts families. It divides churches. It is like rat poison. It smells and looks good, but it ultimately kills its victim. Although sin often brings short-term pleasure, if not atoned for, it terminates in *infinite* pain.

God is holy. How could he be infinitely good and apathetic toward evil at the same time? Infinite goodness must aggressively hate everything that destroys happiness. This is the best way to understand the perfections of God's wrath. God is angry about the source of all suffering and pain—sin—and we are thankful that he is.

WRATH AT THE CROSS

All of this means that the Father's wrath is a virtue. When Christ bore our sin on the cross, the Father punished his Son in our place. He poured out his anger, so richly deserved by us, on his Son. The cross was a vehicle to express God's wrath, and God wanted it expressed. "What the cross tells us is that God hates sin," notes Dr. Martyn Lloyd-Jones. "God is the eternal antithesis of sin. God abominates sin with the whole intensity of His divine and perfect and holy nature. And God not only hates sin, he cannot tolerate it. God cannot compromise with sin."[12]

When God poured out his wrath on his Son, it appeared in many ways. First, the Jewish people rejected Jesus. They asked for Barabbas, a common criminal, and rejected perfection, crying, "Crucify, crucify him!" (Luke 23:21). It appeared as pain. The Roman soldiers pounded a thorny crown into Christ's head. They viciously scourged him. God's wrath appeared as ridicule. They mocked him, jeered at him, and made fun of him. It appeared as humiliation. The Roman soldiers stripped him naked and crucified him in that condition. It appeared as excruciating, tortured pain. They nailed him to a cross. Then they retreated to dispassionately watch him suffer a slow, tormented death.

The amazing truth is this: It was his Father's doing. God the Father worked through the Jews and the Roman soldiers to ensure that the holy wrath of God himself was fully expressed. "It was the will of the LORD to crush him; he [the Father] has put him [the Son] to grief" (Isa. 53:10).

"Never did God so manifest his hatred of sin as in the death and suffering of his only-begotten Son," wrote Jonathan Edwards. "Hereby he showed himself unappeasable to sin, and that it was impossible for him to be at peace with it."[13]

Calvary paints an unpopular picture. Through the megaphone of his Son's suffering, God shouts this message: "I hate evil in every form. It deserves my intense anger. My anger must be poured out on sin before I can forgive. My holy wrath must find expression."

The cross leads us to this conclusion: There are only two types of people. There are those who put their faith in Jesus and let him bear God's wrath in their place. And there are those who try to earn salvation on their own terms. They will bear this wrath themselves, in hell, for eternity.

These truths are very sobering to parents. They sensitize us to sin. They motivate us to take our children's heart-sins seriously. They motivate us to take parenting seriously. Success or failure has ominous consequences.

CONCLUSION

The content of this chapter should affect perceptive parents.

First, chapter 3 suggested that the fear of God is the key to effective parenting. What the cross teaches us about God's holiness provokes Christian parents to fear God. As we have seen, the greatest display of God's holiness is not in the Old Testament. It is in the New Testament. It is at the cross. What transpired at the cross, properly understood, is the reason to fear God.

The fear of God is an important result of the gospel. Revelation 14:6 reads: "Then I saw another angel flying directly overhead, with an eternal gospel to proclaim to those who dwell on earth, to every nation and tribe and language and people." We expect to hear the angel proclaim Christ's death and resurrection. Instead, the angel proclaims this message: "Fear God and give him glory" (Rev. 14:7). He says this because the fear of God and giving glory to God are both effects of the gospel.

Second, the cross motivates Christian parents to pursue their own personal holiness. The cross sets us apart. Like God, our ways become different from the ways of non-Christians. We do things differently. Secular media and the public schools no longer set our parenting agenda; the Bible does.

The knowledge of God's holiness equips us to increasingly *feel* the eternal consequences of sin. As we will see in the next chapter, God's love of virtue, especially his humility and servanthood, is impossible to understand apart from a thorough acquaintance with God's holiness. All of this profoundly affects our approach to parenting.

The cross motivates parents to hate sin, first in themselves, then in their children. To the parents apathetic and passive about their own sin, and by extension their children's, the cross says, "God takes this very seriously. You need to get serious about changing." The cross says, "God is not like you. He hates sin with all his being. He sees its destructive nature. It provokes his anger. He is not passive. Unresisted sin will eventually destroy you and your children. God will never be at peace with it. It will be punished either at the cross or in you or your child with eternal conscious torment."

Third, the cross gives us an eternal perspective. In the second chapter I suggested that Christian parents raise their children with eternity in view. The realities of the cross sensitize us to who it is we and our children will someday stand before in judgment. He is holy. For this reason no one can see him and live. He dwells in unapproachable light (1 Tim. 6:16). Our job is to prepare our children to see him face to face, and clothed in Christ's righteousness, joyfully stand forever.

Fourth, the holiness of God, demonstrated at the cross, makes parents decisive. The cross reshapes vague, fuzzy thinking. It becomes sharp-cornered and edgy. The cross teaches parents to never presume upon the grace of God. The cross motivates the passive parent to decisive action.

Fifth, the holiness of God, demonstrated at the cross, makes both parents and children needy. It convinces us that salvation cannot be earned. It motivates us to joyfully pursue our salvation in Christ alone.

In their book *How People Change*, Lane and Tripp insightfully write: "One of the reasons teenagers are not excited by the gospel is that they do not think they need it. Many parents have successfully raised self-righteous little Pharisees. When they look at themselves, they do not see a sinner in desperate need, so they are not grateful for a Savior."[14] Children raised by diligent parents immersed in the holiness of God are not apt to share this problem.

These five benefits can be summed up with one phrase—the fear of God. "But this is the one to whom I will look: he who is humble and contrite in spirit and trembles at my word" (Isa. 66:2). The fear of God introduces us to these three virtues. It humbles us. It motivates contrition and trembling at God's Word. God looks at the parents with these virtues and blesses their efforts.

Chapter 3 examined some of the lavish promises to parents who fear God. The cross convinces us that God is holy. The fear of God is a by-product of living at the foot of the cross. Blessed is the child whose parents possess it.

We are now ready to plunge into the depths of God's infinite grace. What makes God's grace so wonderful is that it is holy grace. Unless the grace of God is firmly planted in the fear of God, it will bear little fruit in our parenting. God's amazing grace is the subject of the next chapter.

STUDY QUESTIONS

1. In your own words, try to sum up the contents of this chapter.

2. This chapter suggests that theology is more important than technique. How should the theology discussed in this chapter shape parenting?

3. God the Father is holy. He separates himself from sin. His ways are separate from the world's ways. How should this idea impact parenting?

4. In what practical ways should the knowledge of God's holiness motivate Christians to parent their children differently?

5. It is often said that a parent should never discipline a child when angry. In light of this chapter, do you think that is true? Why or why not? (Hint: Read Ephesians 4:26.)

6. In what way will the knowledge of God's holiness, his hatred of evil, and his anger toward evil change your approach to parenting?

5

A GRACIOUS FATHER

THE PREVIOUS CHAPTER discussed God's transcendence. He is different from us. God is holy. He hates evil. But God is not just transcendent. He is also immanent. He is close to his children. He loves them. He pursues a relationship with them. "The LORD is merciful and gracious," wrote David, "slow to anger and abounding in steadfast love" (Ps. 103:8).

God adopts us into his family by grace through faith. We don't get in by performing. God's family, God's fatherhood, is all about grace. And what makes God's grace so wonderful is that it is *holy* grace.

Grace is the heart and soul of Christianity. It is what makes Christianity different from every other religion. Salvation cannot be earned. It is a gift. All other religions work for salvation. Hindus must pass through numerous reincarnations. Jews and Muslims obey law. Evil spirits enslave animists, who must constantly work to please them. But true salvation is the *gracious* gift of an infinitely holy God. Therefore, those who understand and exult in grace have cut right to the heart and soul of Christianity. Grace is fundamental to God's family. It is the air his children breathe. It is crucial to parenting.

Those who see what their adoption cost God, in light of what they deserve, are stunned and amazed by God's grace. It is holy grace. It is not common.

For most Americans, *grace* is a synonym for kindness, charm, or good manners. When I used to think of grace, a Southern belle with impeccable social skills came to mind. She did not offend. She pleased. She was smooth.

Grace is unmerited favor, and it is absolutely holy. Many use the acronym G.R.A.C.E. to define it—God's Riches At Christ's Expense. Although everything in this definition is true, it does not really take us to the heart and soul of grace. Why? It says nothing about what we deserve. We appreciate and value grace to the degree that we understand what we deserve. Therefore, for this acronym to work, we must figure the ugliness of our sin into the equation. If the definition read, "G.R.A.C.E. is God's Riches At Christ's Expense *extended to men and women who by nature deserve wrath*," we would have a complete definition of *grace*.

Wrath introduces us to grace. The holiness of God, discussed in the previous chapter, must precede this chapter. John Frame says it this way: Grace is God's "sovereign, unmerited favor, given to those who deserve his wrath."[1] In his *New Testament Commentary* William Hendriksen adds, "God's grace is his active favor bestowing the greatest gift upon those who have deserved the greatest punishment."[2] "Grace is favor shown to people who do not deserve any favor at all," concludes Martyn Lloyd-Jones. "We deserve nothing but hell. If you think you deserve heaven, take it from me, you are not a Christian."[3]

Even well-known Christian leaders are confused about grace. A friend attended a Christian women's conference. Ten thousand were present. Although the theme was grace, no one defined it. So a moderator asked a panel of conference leaders for a public definition. There was a long pause. "Grace is empowerment," the keynote speaker answered.

Grace does include empowerment (by the Holy Spirit), but this is not the heart of it. It is something much richer. Since it is a topic of such confusion, the rest of this chapter will attempt to unpack it.

GOD IS GRACIOUS

To see the holiness of God's grace clearly, we need to unwrap the word *unmerited*. We can say it this way: Grace is reward, or favor, given to those who *deserve judgment*. If a judge found a serial rapist guilty, and then stepped down from his bench, agreed to take the death penalty in the criminal's place, and sent the rapist on an all-expense-paid vacation to Hawaii for thirty years, that would be grace. The severity of the criminal's crimes would be the measure of the judge's grace. In the same way, the knowledge of what we deserve, and what it cost God to be gracious, is the measure of his fatherly grace. When all is said and done, the cross is the tape that measures the length and breadth of God's grace. Like God's wrath, his grace is holy. It transcends all human conceptions.

The cross proclaims what we deserve. It was an exchange. The offended judge, the Father, sent his innocent Son to take our punishment. He was our substitute in punishment. He did this in order to give us the reward that Christ deserves. "For our sake," Paul wrote, "he made him to be sin who knew no sin, so that in him we might become the righteousness of God" (2 Cor. 5:21).

Think about it. This means that sinners who deserve crucifixion instead get the reward that *perfection* deserves. We get it at God's *expense*, and there is absolutely nothing we can do to earn or repay this exchange. This should stun us! It should astonish us! Most importantly, it should deeply and profoundly humble us.

As a pastor I have discovered that many Christians are not clear on grace. I never presume that anyone understands the gospel of the grace of God, no matter how long the person has attended church. So let's pause to define *grace* and unravel it with five important propositions. You will need to internalize them to be an effective parent.

GOD IS FREE

Our first proposition is that God is free. This means that he is free not to be gracious. The only thing God owes us is justice! He does not owe us grace. We are sinners. We have no claim on God's grace. This means that if God is not gracious, no one can say, "That is not fair." Why? Because fairness implies obligation, but God is not obligated to be gracious.

90

We know this because God withheld grace from the fallen angels. He did not owe it to them. He gave them what he owed them: justice. "God did not spare angels when they sinned, but cast them into hell and committed them to chains of gloomy darkness to be kept until the judgment" (2 Peter 2:4). God did not spare angels. He could have, but he didn't. He did not offer them forgiveness. He did not give them an opportunity for repentance and redemption. He did not give them grace, and this was no blemish on his character.

If this is true, none of us have a claim on grace either. The only thing that God owes us is justice. God could have treated us like the angels. They were sinless before they fell. As far as we know, they committed only one sin. Had God left us in our sins to perish, none of his moral perfections would have been tarnished. "Grace is free," notes J. I. Packer, "in the sense of being self-originated and of proceeding from One who was free not to be gracious. Only when it is seen that what decides each individual's destiny is whether or not God resolves to save him from his sins, and that this is a decision which God need not make in any single case, can one begin to grasp the biblical view of grace."[4]

In summary, God is never obligated to be gracious. He extends grace because he loves sinners. He also loves grace and delights to exercise it. He is free to give it to one and withhold it from another.

GOD HAS NO NEEDS

Second, God has no needs. This means that when he is gracious, it is not to satisfy a need in himself. "Nor is [God] served by human hands, *as though he needed anything*, since he himself gives to all mankind life and breath and everything" (Acts 17:25).

God has no needs because he is completely satisfied in his own inter-Trinitarian community.[5] He is infinitely happy. He is infinitely peaceful. His Spirit is "joy . . . inexpressible and filled with glory" (1 Peter 1:8). He has all knowledge and power. If he were unhappy, he would immediately know why, and would have the power to remedy it on the spot. He lacks no experience of being loved or accepted. He is utterly sufficient in himself.

This means that God did not create us because he lacked fellowship, or because he needed someone to love, or because he was dissatisfied with his relationships in the eternal council of the Godhead (Father, Son, and Holy Spirit). "God is not constrained by any inner deficiency or unhappiness to do anything he does not want to do," notes John Piper. "He has been complete and overflowing with satisfaction from all eternity. He needs no education. No one can offer anything to him that doesn't already come from him."[6]

This presents finite, needy creatures, like us, with a problem. We cannot understand action, especially infinitely costly action, that is not driven by need. We do everything to satisfy needs. We marry because we need companionship. We work because we need money. We have children because we need a posterity. We even love and serve God because we need eternal life. We are empty vessels that need filling. By contrast, God's vessel continually overflows with a superabundant surplus.

The question remains: If God has no need, why did he create and redeem? The answer is simple. God created to glorify his goodness. He created a context to display and exercise his moral perfections. We exist for God's glory. We exist because God's goodness is constantly overflowing, and he wants to display it and share it.[7]

So, in summary, we have said two things. Not only is God free to not give grace, but when he is gracious it is never to meet a need in himself. This means that only infinite goodness, not any form of selfish self-interest, motivates him to adopt us into his family.

SIN IS INFINITELY OFFENSIVE

Our third proposition concerns our demerit. Not only is God free and without need, but the depth of our demerit is impossible for us to fully understand. God is gracious to enemies, not friends (Rom. 5:8). If we were friends, the "favor" would be "merited," and it wouldn't be grace. As we have already said, the more we understand our enmity toward God, and God's enmity toward us, the more amazing grace becomes.

We discussed God's justice in the previous chapter. We must return to this subject to understand our demerit. God is perfectly just. "The King in his might loves justice" (Ps. 99:4). "The LORD is a God of justice" (Isa. 30:18). He never punishes too harshly. Rather, every sin gets exactly what it deserves and nothing more. God never relaxes justice. To do so would be sin. Instead, he always executes justice. With this foundation in mind, we learn that two truths highlight the enormity of our sin—hell and the cross.

First, hell dramatizes our demerit. It lets us see sin through God's eyes. Hell says that our sin is infinitely heinous in God's sight. Why? Here is the answer: Hell is eternal, conscious torment. "Then he will say to those on his left, 'Depart from me, you cursed, into the *eternal fire* prepared for the devil and his angels" (Matt. 25:41).[8] Although unredeemed sinners suffer forever, their sin is so serious that their suffering never atones for their sin. No matter how long one stays in hell, the person can never suffer enough to balance the scales of justice and work his or her way back to heaven. So what do hell's torments say about our sin? Since God is infinitely just, they tell us that sin must be infinitely offensive to God. If this were not the case, the existence of eternal conscious torment (hell) would be unjust and God would not be a just judge. "Infinitely offensive sin" is a strong statement. It is hard to swallow. Most of you will want more proof. We have it in the gospel, specifically the cross.

The cross confirms all that we have said about the infinite offense of sin. It says that no finite sacrifice can atone for sin (Heb. 10:4). Nothing but a sacrifice of infinite value, God himself, can atone for our offenses. In addition, no one but an infinite Being is capable of suffering sufficiently to atone for infinite offenses against an infinitely holy God.

That is why Jesus had to be God. A human sacrifice could not get the job done. If he was only human, you and I are still dead in our sins. An object of finite value cannot atone for sins infinitely offensive. Only a sacrifice of infinite value can right the scales of divine justice and secure our forgiveness. Bridges and Bevington concur. "The atonement could only be the work of a divine person of infinite worth and dignity

94

since the offense of our sins against a holy God is an infinitely appalling atrocity."[9]

By sin I am not thinking primarily of adultery, drunkenness, or bank robbing. I am thinking of secret, inner, spiritual sins—a lustful look, a proud, condescending thought, unbelief, selfishness, critical speech, or gossip. Remember, all Adam and Eve did was to bite into a forbidden apple. They didn't commit adultery or snort cocaine. Yet the result was death, suffering, alienation, and rejection for billions. Can we fully comprehend the horror of sin? Is it possible for us to ever really see it from God's perspective?

Therefore, we conclude that we can't even begin to understand how God hates our sin, how it alienates us from him, how it rightfully brings his wrath upon us.

I have said all of this to make this point: *It is to enemies that God sends grace,* and he sends this grace despite the fact that nothing in the recipients of his grace compels him to be gracious, nor does any need motivate him. Truly, God's grace is holy. It is utterly amazing!

WE ARE HELPLESS

Our fourth proposition is that you and I are helpless. If what I have said so far is true, then this should be self-evident. Yet most people have no knowledge of their helplessness. In fact, most people (even many professing Christians) think that people get into heaven by being good.

At a recent funeral the husband of the deceased turned to me with tears in his eyes and said, "My wife was an unusually good person. If anyone can get into heaven, she will." This man is a professing Christian. He has gone to church every Sunday for eighty years. But he doesn't have the slightest clue about his helplessness. He has no understanding of his sin, God's holiness, or God's grace.

I often shock my congregation by saying, "Virtue keeps more people out of heaven than all their sins combined." After my listeners recover, I explain. "What I mean is that *confidence* in our virtues keeps more people out of heaven than all their adultery and drunkenness combined." We cannot be good enough. We will never meet God's standards. To please God, we must confess our bankruptcy. "None is righteous, no, not one. . . . All have turned aside; together they have become worthless; *no one does good, not even one*" (Rom. 3:10, 12, quoting Ps. 14:1, 3). We cannot be good enough because God requires perfection. "No one is perfect" is one of the most common expressions in the English language. That's the problem. We must be perfect.

Many Christians and non-Christians do good deeds. Many non-Christians care for the sick and serve in soup kitchens. Audrey Hepburn spent the last years of her life serving children in Third World countries. Paul is not saying that people do not do good deeds. He is saying that unless these deeds are done with faith toward God and for the glory of God, they earn no merit with God. It is not enough to do good things. The deed must proceed from holy motives. That is why we conclude that no one can earn heaven. It is utterly impossible.

If this is true, trying a little harder is a waste of time. If this is true, all the altruistic Buddhists, Muslims, and Latter-day

Saints are in deep trouble. If this is true, New Year's resolutions are smoke and mirrors.

God's Son came to earth and suffered infinite pains precisely because we are helpless. Christians are those who confess, "Our situation is and was helpless." In fact, reliance on our virtues is not a neutral issue. It is deep sin. It makes God angry. Why? Attempts to be "good enough" reject Christ, his cross, and his atoning work. If you sent your son to be tortured to death for friends because their situation was helpless and they said, "Thanks, but no thanks. I can work it out on my own," how would you feel? You would not be happy.

Conversing with a Christian friend who believed he needed to perform to be acceptable to God, I said, "Those who seek God's acceptance through performance reject the cross of Christ, and I know you don't want to do that." He became very upset with me. He was convinced that God was pleased with his attempts to merit salvation. He was angry at the suggestion that his attempts to merit God's favor were in fact a rejection of the cross. But listen to this strong language: "For all who rely on works of the law [that is, trying a little harder] are under a curse; for it is written, 'Cursed be everyone who does not abide by all things written in the Book of the Law, and do them'" (Gal. 3:10, quoting Deut. 27:26); "You are severed from Christ, you who would be justified by the law; you have fallen away from grace" (Gal. 5:4). That is how Paul describes those who trust in their own virtues—cursed and severed from Christ.

In summary, if you believe all the basic Christian truths, but you persist in trying to get right with God by being good, you inadvertently reject the gospel. The truth is, we are helpless. We appropriate the power of the gospel through faith by God's grace, not by working. "By grace you have been saved through faith. And this is not your own doing; it is the gift of God, not a result of works, so that no one might boast" (Eph. 2:8–9).

We have made four points: God is free. God is without need. We are God's enemies. And we are helpless to change our predicament through human effort.

THE COST OF GRACE TO GOD

Our fifth and last proposition is this: My capacity to understand grace will always be a function of my understanding of what it cost the Father to be gracious. When salvation occurs, the Father adopts us into his family. He makes us his sons and daughters.

Adoptions in this world are expensive. I heard of a Christian who paid thirty thousand dollars to adopt a child from China. Yet this is low budget compared to what the Father paid to adopt you and me. The cost was infinite.

Imagine this scenario. A poor father takes his ten-year-old son into his lap. "It is time for me to tell you the truth. You are not our birth child. We adopted you when you were six weeks old. At one time my estate was worth ten million dollars, but we wanted you in our family so much that we spent our entire fortune on your adoption. We have been poor ever since, but we have never regretted it. Your presence in our family has been worth more than all the money in the world."

How do you think this child would feel? His first response would probably be disappointment: "This is not my real father." But his second response would be joy, the deep joy of knowing he was actually loved, valued, maybe esteemed even more than most birth children. Why would he feel this way? The knowledge of the cost of his adoption would be the measure of his father's love.

This is how God's grace should affect us. The cost of our adoption was not ten million dollars. *It was infinite.* As we have seen, it took a sacrifice of infinite value to atone for infinite offenses that were infinitely heinous to an infinitely holy God.

This is what transpired at the cross. God gave us that which he loved infinitely, his greatest treasure, his Son, to secure our adoption. Think of this in the context of our first four propositions. The Father paid this price in the absence of any obligation to us, in the absence of any need in himself, despite infinite enmity toward us, and despite our utter helplessness. He did it because he loves us. He did it to exercise grace. He did it to glorify his grace.

God's grace is off the charts. It is not like this world's grace. Love motivated it. No wonder Paul prayed that we "may have strength to comprehend with all the saints what is the breadth and length and height and depth, and to know the love of Christ that *surpasses knowledge,* that you may be filled with all the fullness of God" (Eph. 3:18–19).

In conclusion, grace is not just "unmerited favor." We need to go further. It is reward given to those who deserve punishment. We will spend the rest of our lives growing in the knowledge of this grace (Eph. 1:6). It will be our greatest joy and praise.

FRUIT OF GRACE

We are making the point that God's family is all about grace. This has big implications for parenting. Christians do not work to get grace. They work because they have received grace. Christians do not earn God's favor. They serve because God has already shown them favor. Christians do not work to merit salvation. They joyfully serve God because he has already given them salvation.

As we have noted, grace is one of the great chasms between Christianity and every other religion. The default condition of the human heart is "be good enough and God will accept you." Iain Murray notes that "the religion of the natural man is always a religion of self-righteousness."[10]

Christianity reverses all of this. It says, "God accepts you despite the fact that you have angered him with an infinite offense. God accepts you even though you must be perfect, but you cannot be. God sent his Son to do what you cannot. He lived a perfect life in your place. He bore the Father's just wrath for your infinitely heinous sins. He did this despite the fact that it would have been completely just for him to leave you in your sins. He did this despite any lack of need in himself. His only motive was sheer, overwhelming, incomprehensible love."

All Christian obedience and service (including parenting) is a response to this amazing grace. It is a response to what Paul called "the gospel of the grace of God" (Acts 20:24). Yet unfortunately, there are other motives. Pride motivates many Christian parents. We want to look good to others. Sometimes, deep down inside, we parent to show that we are God's equal. No free gifts. He must be repaid. At other times, guilt motivates our parenting. "If I do such and such, he will forgive me." Insecurity motivates others. "Compared to _____, I am a slouch. If I were like _____, then surely God would love me." Finally, fear is often a motivation. "Surely God will punish me if I don't perform, if I don't measure up."

By contrast, those who see and feel God's grace respond with joy and gratitude. They seek to be like God in holiness and godliness, not to earn his favor, but because his grace has captured their hearts. They see the moral beauty of God, and they want to be like him. They see what God has done for them. They offer their lives in joyful gratitude. Grace motivates us to love God. Grace makes us increasingly humble. Grace motivates us to obey God. Grace motivates us to love our brothers and sisters. It alone produces the good works that God seeks. Grace also motivates effective parenting.

CONCLUSION

This book is about how the gospel impacts parenting. How should the grace of God affect parents?

First, it should convince us that our pretensions to parental perfection are futile. It reminds us every day that we cannot be perfect. We can't discipline consistently. We can't teach sufficiently. We don't love adequately. But it also emboldens us. It reminds us that God's grace is perfected in our weakness (2 Cor. 12:9–10).

Second, the grace of God makes parents increasingly sincere, gracious, and humble. When we discipline inappropriately, or set a bad example, God's grace and kindness prompt us to confess our failings to our spouse and children. When we discipline inappropriately, God's grace compels us to ask our children's forgiveness. When we treat our spouse uncharitably in front of our children, God's grace motivates us to seek our children's forgiveness.

Parents who see God's grace this way are gracious to their children. This does not mean that they shirk their responsibility to discipline. Rather, they administer God's discipline with the tenderness and compassion of those who see their own sins and failings crucified, judged, and punished in Christ at the cross. When they discipline, Paul's words are always before them: "Brothers, if anyone is caught in any transgression, you who are spiritual should restore him in a spirit of gentleness. Keep watch on yourself, lest you too be tempted" (Gal. 6:1).

Third, the grace of God motivates us to love our spouse and our children sacrificially. This is the subject of chapter 11. It prompts mothers to put their families before their careers. If a mom's career is hurting her children, and she sees God's grace extended to herself from the cross, she will be motivated to die to her selfish ambition for the good of her children.

It motivates fathers to put their wives and children before careers or hobbies. The bottom line is this: You can't understand God's grace extended to you and not want to extend it to others.

SUMMARY OF CHAPTERS 3 THROUGH 5

Chapter 3 emphasized the truth that God blesses the child whose parents fear God. Chapter 4 argued the Father's holiness, and chapter 5 his graciousness. At the cross, we learn to fear God in a wholesome, life-giving way. There God demonstrates his holiness, his justice, his wrath, his love, and his grace.

Those who fear God discipline their children, they teach them, they set a godly example for them, and they lavish them with love. The prophets promised that the New Covenant would teach us this fear. "I will give them one heart and one way, that they may fear me forever, for their own good and the good of their children after them" (Jer. 32:39). We learn this fear at the cross.

Blessed are the children whose parents learn to fear this holy, wonderful God. They alone know what Jerry Bridges calls the joy of fearing God.[11]

The next six chapters are going to apply the cross, the heart of the gospel, and its ensuing fear to the tools of parenting: the example of the parents' marriage, the husband's role in parenting, the importance of disciplining children, the need to teach our children, and the need to lavish our children with affection.

STUDY QUESTIONS

1. How did this chapter change your definition of *grace?*

2. Why was chapter 4 a necessary precedent to understanding this chapter?

3. To understand God's grace, you need to understand God's freedom to not be gracious, his lack of need, the infinite offense of your sin, your helplessness, and what it cost

God to be gracious to you. Which of these ideas was new? Which most deeply affected you?

4. There are many motivations for serving Christ—fear, guilt, insecurity, pride, and grace. Which of these motivates you most frequently? What would a Christian look like if that person were motivated by nothing but the grace of God? How can we motivate our children with grace?

5. This chapter discussed two distortions of grace—presumption and legalism. Which are you most prone to? Why?

6. How should the contents of this chapter affect your parenting?

6

THE FIRST PRINCIPLE
OF PARENTING

FRANK AND KIM have been married for thirty years. They raised four beautiful children, but their marriage was a spiritual battleground.

Frank was harsh with Kim. He took her for granted. He was unaffectionate. He seldom communicated with her. He often looked down on her. The truth is, in his eyes she was never good enough. Finally, Kim rebelled. She quit cleaning the house. She quit cooking. She withdrew both emotionally and relationally.

Frank and Kim tried to compensate with their children. Daily they rose early to teach them the Bible. The family went to church every Sunday. There the children heard the gospel on a regular basis. The couple invested thousands in the best private Christian education. They scrupulously protected their children from the negative influences of the outside world. They tried everything in the book except the one thing that really mattered—their marriage.

Now the children are grown. Three have stopped going to church. One is a church attender, but his heart is not in it. What went wrong? Frank and Kim's marriage preached an unattractive gospel to their children. It contradicted the gospel preached at church and school.

The marriage of Stephen and Melody was different. Stephen was warm and loving. He did his best to provide spiritual leadership for his wife and children. Melody tried, albeit imperfectly, to support him. Like every couple they had their disagreements, but they always settled scores quickly and forgave each other from the heart. Stephen made it a practice to apologize to his children when he mistreated his wife in front of them. He understood the power of example and wielded it effectively.

They went to Frank and Kim's church. And although their three children attended public schools, all married committed Christians and serve God joyfully today.

The story of these marriages makes a point. God speaks through our example. There is an old proverb: "Children learn more by the eye than they do by the ear." The most important example that parents possess is their marriage. Our marriages preach. They preach a message that either attracts or repels our children.

Parents who joyfully pursue God are contagious. Joyful sacrifice for the gospel is contagious. A gospel that makes parents stable, sincere, joyful, loving, affectionate, and humble is contagious. Children will want a God that produces these qualities.

On the other hand, parents going through the motions of church, enslaved to rules, serving God to gain his acceptance, tolerating their spouses, or worse, engaging in open warfare, chase their children away from God and his church. When Mom and Dad preach one thing but do the opposite, and don't repent to their children, it makes the world attractive and the gospel irrelevant.

Kids also internalize their parents' passions. They alone see what or who you *really* love, and not what you merely pretend to love. Maybe it is upward mobility. Maybe your passion is entertainment (sports, movies, music). For others it is hunting, shopping, or golf.

If you ask parents what is the most important thing they can do to raise children who will follow Christ, some will mention adequate discipline, others enrollment in a Christian school, still others the importance of home-schooling or Bible reading. They rarely mention example. Yet example is the first principle of parenting. This should not surprise us. Parenting is about leadership, and example is the first principle of biblical leadership. When parents practice what they teach, God gives them moral authority in their children's eyes. All teaching in the Bible starts with example.

THE POWER OF EXAMPLE

Jesus taught by example. "In the first book, O Theophilus, I have dealt with all that Jesus began *to do and teach*" (Acts 1:1). Notice the sequence. First Jesus did, then he taught. Every effective parent does likewise. Children seldom internalize the teaching of hypocrites. But the teaching of those who live what they preach pierces deeply into our children's hearts.

Jesus is the only person who did this perfectly. He told his disciples to take up their cross because he took up his cross (Matt. 16:24–25). Jesus told his disciples to humble themselves because he humbled himself (Phil. 2:5–8). Jesus told his followers to obey the Father because he obeyed his Father (John 8:29; Phil. 2:8). There was a perfect correlation between what Jesus taught and what he did. He was God's only perfect leader.[1]

"Whatever the leaders are, the people become," notes John MacArthur. "Biblical history demonstrates that people will seldom rise above the spiritual level of their leadership."[2] Dave Harvey adds, "True leadership models its message. . . . A leader proclaims with two voices: one through lips, the other through life. . . . Together, these messages converge to create a solid platform of credibility and stature."[3]

Here is my point: Parenting is the most important leadership position in the church. And example is also the first principle of parenting. Parents lead the family, the smallest and most important cell in the local church. Archbishop Tillotson (1630–94) said, "To give children good instruction, and a bad example, is but beckoning to them with the head to show them the way to heaven, while we take them by the hand and lead them in the way to hell."[4]

I have said all of this to bring us to this point: Our marriage is the most powerful example that we possess. To the degree that the gospel makes our marriage attractive, God will empower us to reach our children. This chapter is going to discuss two important, closely related examples. The first is the example of our marriage. The second is the example of our humility, or, negatively, our pride.

THE MARRIAGE THAT PREACHES GOOD NEWS

Ephesians chapter 5 is the blueprint for marriage. In these verses God gives us clear marching orders.

> Wives, submit to your own husbands, as to the Lord. For the husband is the head of the wife even as Christ is the head of the church, his body, and is himself its Savior. Now as the church submits to Christ, so also wives should submit in everything to their husbands.
>
> Husbands, love your wives, as Christ loved the church and gave himself up for her, that he might sanctify her, having cleansed her by the washing of water with the word, so that he might present the church to himself in splendor, without spot or wrinkle or any such thing, that she might be holy and without blemish. In the same way husbands should love their wives as their own bodies. He who loves his wife loves himself. For no one ever hated his own flesh, but nourishes and cherishes it, just as Christ does the church, because we are members of his body. "Therefore a man shall leave his father and mother and hold fast to his wife, and the two shall become one flesh." *This mystery is profound, and I am saying that it refers to Christ and the church.* However, let each one of you love his wife as himself, and let the wife see that she respects her husband. (Eph. 5:22–33, quoting Gen. 2:24)

I have been stressing the truth that marriage preaches the gospel. Verse 32 makes that principle clear: "This mystery [marriage] is profound, and I am saying that it refers to *Christ and the church*." Here is Paul's point. From before time began, God had marriage on his mind. He was preparing a bride for his Son, whom he would marry forever. It would take the crucifixion and resurrection of the Groom to bring this marriage to pass. Think of it. God created the most intimate human relationship, marriage, to speak of the intimacy of his relationship with his church.

God created the institution of human marriage to reflect, or mirror forth, this eternal union. In other words, human marriage exists to point men and angels to the eternal marriage of Christ and his church. The gospel made this divine marriage possible. Here is our point: human marriage exists to preach the gospel. It exists to illustrate the fruit that should follow the preaching of the gospel in the church.

To whom do our marriages preach? Of course, the first audience is God and his angels. They watch and rejoice, or if our marriage is a war zone, they grieve.

Who is the second audience? Most of us think first about our non-Christian neighbors. Maybe they will see our attempts to model Christian marriage and want the gospel? They might, and we hope they will, but actually they are the third audience.

The second audience, usually overlooked by most Christians, is our children. What is our marriage telling them about Christ and his bride? They see it all. They hear our fights. They absorb our attitudes. They know who or what really sits on the throne of our lives. They watch how we handle resentment. They hear the way we talk to each other. They know when we hear the Sunday sermon and apply it. They also know when we ignore it.

The message that our marriage preaches either repels or attracts our children. God wants your child to watch your marriage and think, "I want a marriage like that, and I want the God that produced it." Or, "When I think of the beauty of the gospel, I think of my parents' marriage. I want to be part of a church that is loved by God the way my dad loves my mother. I want to be part of a church that finds its joy in submitting to Christ as my mother joyfully submits to my father."

The gospel is the good news that the Groom loves his bride. He loved her so much that he humbled himself, descended an infinite distance, became man, and suffered poverty and abuse for thirty-three years. Then, in the greatest display of love in history, he allowed himself to be tortured to death on a cross in his bride's place. The Son of God did all of this to serve his bride, to make peace where enmity reigned. What motivated him? Love that surpasses knowledge! He longed to unite himself in irrevocable love to an unworthy bride.

But the gospel is not just about the Groom's love. It also provokes a response from his bride. When understood from the heart, it motivates her to humble herself, love the Groom with all her heart, respect him, and serve him with joyful abandon. The gospel summons Christ's bride to yield to the servant authority of her crucified King.

Here is Paul's point: Christian marriage preaches this union. It makes it either attractive or ugly. When a husband loves his wife as Christ loves the church, washing her with the Word, forgiving her, serving her, and tenderly leading her, his marriage says, "Christ loves his church. You can trust the Groom. He is infinitely loving. Serve him. You won't be disappointed."

111

When a husband humbly loves a menopausal (or premenstrual) wife, his behavior says, "Christ loves the church even though she is sinful." His behavior tells his children, "Christ loves his bride even when she is unattractive." It says that nothing can separate us from the love of Christ, even our failings.

But when a husband is unfaithful to his wife, verbally belittles her, loves his children more than her, or takes her for granted, his marriage says, "Christ's love is not that great. He loves us only when we perform. You can't trust this Savior. You can't meet his expectations. He doesn't keep his promises. Why serve a fickle despot?" His deeds say, "Many things can separate us from the love of Christ."

Wives also preach. When Mom joyfully submits to her husband "*as to the Lord*" (Eph. 5:22), recognizing that he is her head as Christ is the Head of the church, and that she is his body as the church is the body of Christ, it makes an attractive statement. When she does this for an unworthy husband, not because she trusts *him*, but because she trusts Christ to care for her, it points her children to Christ. Her behavior says, "Christ is trustworthy." It says, "The Son of God is infinitely good. You can trust him. My father is very imperfect, but Mom trusts Christ to take care of her. If she can trust Jesus this way, I can also."

But when a wife tells her children to obey Christ, yet doesn't trust him enough to take care of her relationship with an imperfect husband, but seeks to control him, resists his authority, refuses to respect him, and declines to serve him, her actions speak loudly. They say, "The Son of God cannot be trusted. He promises to exalt the humble, but I don't believe he will exalt me. He says he will take care of those who submit to lawful authority, but I don't really believe that. If I don't take care of myself, who will?" In most cases her children will internalize what she does, not what she says.

What I am saying is that our marriages exist for something bigger than themselves, and our children are watching. Christ's marriage to his church greatly surpasses our human marriages. Ours are temporary. They end with death. In the new heaven and earth there will be no marriage or giving in marriage (Matt. 22:29–30). By contrast, the marriage of Christ to his church is eternal. It will never end. Ultimately, only one marriage remains—the marriage of Christ to his bride.

This principle is especially important for homeschooling moms. With their children all day, they face a great temptation to center their lives and affections on their children. Convinced that it is what they do, or don't do, with their children that will prove decisive, they make their children the center of their lives and affections.

I contend that it is how they love their husbands that will ultimately prove decisive. In other words, marriage-centered, not child-centered, moms usually exert the greatest influence on their children for Christ and his kingdom. This means that your weekends away with your husband, alone, might influence your children more than all your teaching and disciplining combined. Your children are watching, and it gives them great joy and security to see their parents loving each other.

In summary, how we conduct our marriages communicates what we really think about Christ's marriage to his church, which is the fruit of the gospel.

Fig. 3. God in a successful marriage

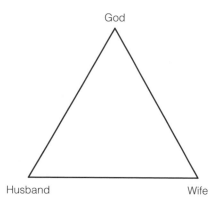

What can we do to obtain marriages like this? First, deepen your relationship with God. The closer Mom and Dad get to God, the closer they usually get to each other (see Figure 3). Notice that as Mom and Dad move up the triangle toward God, they move closer to each other. I have never seen an exception to this principle. Parents who pray and study the Bible in secret grow increasingly close to God. The result is deeper communion with each other and a stronger example for their children.

Second, pray together as a couple. I don't mean as you are falling asleep in bed at night. It must occupy a higher priority in your life than that. Do you pray together, just the two of you, on a regular basis? Couples make their marriage a priority when they pray together. It will not escape their children. Whenever a couple comes to me for marriage counseling, the first thing I ask is, "Do you pray together on a regular basis?" I have never received a positive response from a marriage in trouble. There is an old saying, "Couples that pray together stay together." Couples that pray together work through conflicts together.

THE EXAMPLE-WRECKER

Hypocrisy cripples our parenting example. Hypocrisy occurs whenever we tell our kids to do one thing, and then do the opposite ourselves. Hypocrisy is one of the sins that provokes children to anger. "Fathers, do not provoke your children to anger, but bring them up in the discipline and instruction of the Lord" (Eph. 6:4). In this text, Paul doesn't tell us what provokes children to anger, but hypocrisy has to be at the top of the list.

Behind hypocrisy, pride is usually lurking. Pride is blindness to our faults, sins, and failings. Most importantly, pride is blind to the existence of itself. Therefore, the more proud you are, the more humble you will feel, and the more humble you are, the more proud you will feel. That is because true humility is the opening of the eyes to our personal sin, and one of the first things a humble person becomes aware of is his or her pride.

Here is the problem: Our children see the very sins to which we are blind. They have a front-row seat, and they are watching intently. Pride makes it possible for us to tell our children one thing even while we *unknowingly* do another. Pride blinds us to the contradictions within ourselves, or worse, puffs us up so much that we don't care. The result is hypocrisy, and more than anything else, hypocrisy hardens our children to the message we want them to hear.

Pride has many symptoms. First, proud parents see their children's sins, but they are unable to see the same sins in themselves. In Jesus' words, we try to remove the speck from our child's eye even while we have a log in our own

(Matt. 7:1–5). We command our children to be unselfish even though we are selfish toward our spouse. We urge our children to speak respectfully to each other, and then they listen to us carve up someone else with our tongue. We tell our children to respect their mother, and then we belittle her with disrespectful speech. We exhort our children to be generous even though we don't tithe. The examples are endless.

Second, pride makes us uncorrectable. My wife brings a valid criticism, and the first thing I do is to rise to my defense. I do this because protecting myself is more important to me than discovering the truth about myself so that I can change wrong behavior. This tells my children that I really have little interest in personal holiness. Proud parents cannot hear correction from their children either. They are unapproachable, and their children know it. Such parents will not admit wrongdoing because their self-opinion is too high. Even if they become aware of their failings, they are too proud to confess them. While we are busy preserving our self-respect, we are losing it in our children's eyes.

The greater our pride, the greater our capacity to teach one thing and do the opposite, completely unaware of our hypocrisy. Because our children are proud also, they will be able to see our sins completely unaware of the same sin in themselves. Proud parents are ill equipped to help their children escape the clutches of pride.

Here is the point: Pride, manifesting itself as hypocrisy, provokes children to anger. It discourages them. It closes their ears to our instruction. It makes their hearts stony ground, where the gospel cannot take root (Matt. 13:18–21). When Mom invests herself in her career selfishly, at the expense of her children, and then expects unselfishness from them, two things happen. First, the children ignore Mom's words and follow her example. Second, they become hardened to her values. When a father takes his family to church each Sunday, pretending that Christ is first in his life, but in reality makes his hobbies number one, his children see it. They grow hard and calloused to church and religion.

There are many examples of this process. Malcolm X was one of the most influential black Americans of the twentieth century. Although his father was a pastor, Malcolm rebelled and became the leader of the Nation of Islam. Why? What went wrong?

In his book *Missing in Action*, Weldon Hardenbrook says,

> There were serious reasons why the young Malcolm couldn't receive the teaching of his father. His father, Earl, had so many rules it was hard for his children to remember them all. But, according to people who knew him, he failed to observe them himself. Biographer Perry Bruce wrote, "In addition to being brutal to his wife and children, he was notoriously unfaithful to Louise (his wife). 'A natural born whoremonger' is what his friend Chester Jones called him. From childhood onward, Malcolm would have great difficulty trying to decide whether to follow the path of virtue his father preached or the path of vice he often practiced."[5]

Malcolm was a gifted leader. He could have (and should have) served Christ. But he forsook Christianity and became a Black Muslim. His father's life preached so loudly that Malcolm could not hear his words. His heart thoroughly hardened to Christianity, and Malcolm turned to Muhammad. Since the 1960s, millions of black men have turned from Christ to Muhammad because of Malcolm X.

But true believers have a better hope. It lies in the gospel. The gospel humbles us, and that humility attracts our children to our teaching.

EMPOWERING EXAMPLE

The gospel makes parents humble. It is the antidote to pride. Chapters 4 and 5 described the gospel. We see ourselves most perfectly at the foot of the cross. Jesus died in our place. He took what we deserve. What do we deserve? We are cosmic traitors who deserve to be slowly tortured to death, naked, while a crowd stands around mocking, jeering, and laughing. Then, in the climax to the scene, God the Father rejects us forever. But Christians never get what they deserve. Jesus took that punishment. We always get better than we deserve. We get what Christ deserves at his expense. That is the very clear message of the cross. All humility begins with this truth.

The gospel opens my eyes to who I really am—"wretched, pitiable, poor, blind, and naked" (Rev. 3:17). "Biblical humility," notes G. A. Pritchard, "is not some self-induced groveling or hang-dog attitude. Biblical humility is seeing ourselves as we are. Humility is a response to beholding the holiness of God."[6]

In addition, attempting to live Ephesians 5 profoundly humbles us. Aware of the importance of example, sincere parents strive to model the gospel—but the harder they try, the more aware of their failings they become. Fathers who really try to love their wives as Christ loved his church discover the depth of their selfishness. Mothers don't understand the depth of their rebellion and unbelief until they try to submit to their husbands "in everything."

So our attempts to live the gospel expose our failings, which in turn amplifies our humility, which in turn makes us attractive to our children. The gospel is the good news that our children do not need perfect examples. They need _humble examples_.

Humility impacts parents in several ways. First, it makes us quick to admit wrongdoing. "The key to the family functioning as a redemptive community," writes Paul David Tripp, "where the Gospel is the glue that holds the family together, is parents who so trust in Christ that they are ready and willing to _confess their faults to their children._"[7] When they sin against their children, humble parents quickly confess it. They confess their parental faults to God first, but they are not afraid to do so in front of their children also.

In the same way, growing humility makes us quick to confess sin to our spouse. Our children are watching. Confession proves our sincerity. It convinces them that we really want to change. It says that God is worth changing for. God exalts the humble. God gives spiritual authority to parents who humble themselves.

Many times I went to my children and asked their forgiveness for my harsh or ungodly treatment of their mother. When they saw me speak critically to Judy, or put her down, I gathered my children and reminded them that my example was crucial and that I was sorry for my sin, and I asked them to forgive me.

119

I was after their hearts. My mistakes, humbly and sincerely confessed, probably did more to win my children for Christ than all my meager virtues combined.

Confession sends a crucial message to our children. It reminds them that, yes, my parents are imperfect, but they are deadly earnest about following Christ, about wanting to change, and about doing things God's way. Failure to confess our faults sends the opposite message. "My parents talk much about Christ, but following him is not really that important to them. They don't walk the talk. They tell us to do one thing, but they do the other. *And when they fail, they go on as if it doesn't matter.*"

Growing humility opens our eyes to our sin. It makes us tender and gracious discipliners of our children. "Brothers, if anyone is caught in any transgression, you who are spiritual should restore him in a spirit of gentleness. Keep watch on yourself, lest you too be tempted. Bear one another's burdens, and so fulfill the law of Christ. For if anyone thinks he is something, when he is nothing, he deceives himself" (Gal. 6:1–3). Humble parents discipline their children "in a spirit of gentleness." They "keep watch on [themselves]," knowing that they can fall, or probably have fallen, into the same sin. Their growing humility retards the "decei[t]" of thinking they are "something, when [they are] nothing."

True humility flows out of a heart broken for its sins and failings. Humble parents attract their children's favor. Most importantly, humble parents attract God's favor. "God opposes the proud, but gives grace to the humble" (James 4:6, quoting Prov. 3:34). One way he gives grace to humble parents is by changing their children's hearts through the miracle of new birth.

We obtain this humility at the foot of the cross. In other words, the gospel makes us humble. There we see the horror of sin, not just the sins of the world, but our own personal sin. In chapter 4 we learned that because our sin is infinitely heinous to God, only a sacrifice of infinite value can atone for it. Is this how you see your sin? Those who meditate on the message of the cross strive for holiness. Their efforts only make them more aware of their failings. This causes them to run to the cross for forgiveness more frequently. It causes them to need the cross more desperately. All of this happens because they feel the weight of their sins more biblically. It culminates in the peace of biblical humility.

SUMMARY

No human marriage meets God's standard No husband loves his wife as Christ loved his church. It is humanly impossible. No wife submits to her husband as the church is supposed to submit to Christ, "in everything" (Eph. 5:24). We all fail. Short of the resurrection, there are no perfect marriages.

On top of that, none of us is adequately humble. We are all proud people trying, by the grace of God, to become increasingly humble. Hypocrisy lurks in us somewhere.

So what should we do?

This chapter has said that our example matters, that our marriages preach the gospel. It has also indicated that the gospel produces the humility that attracts our children. The gospel has another crucial function. It is the place where needy parents go for cleansing and forgiveness. When I am impatient with my wife, I run to the cross for forgiveness. When I treat my wife selfishly or thoughtlessly, in front of my children, I run to the cross for forgiveness. When Judy fails, she goes there also. At the cross we find grace to help us in our time of need (Heb. 4:16).

We also run to the cross for motivation. When I need a model of sacrificial love, I look to the cross. There I see Christ dying for me, his enemy. When my wife needs motivation to submit to a very imperfect husband, one every bit her equal, she looks to the cross. There she sees Christ submitting to his Father, who was every bit his equal. Jesus doesn't complain. He doesn't demand a turn to lead the Trinity. He doesn't try to control his Father. He doesn't try to manipulate him. He just willingly goes to the cross in perfect obedience and dies.

The cross is our salvation from the condemnation of sin. The cross motivates us to be the parents that God wants us to be. The cross motivates us to preach a compelling example to our children. The cross exposes our pride. It humbles us. It shows us who we really are—sinners saved by grace.

Cross-centered parents are imperfect, but they attract their children. And what they attract them to is the gospel.

STUDY QUESTIONS

1. Whose marriage does yours most resemble—the marriage of Frank and Kim, or the marriage of Stephen and Melody? Why?

2. Ephesians 5:32 reads, "This mystery [marriage] is profound, and I am saying that it refers to Christ and the

church." Based on this verse, explain why God instituted human marriage.

3. Read Ephesians 5:22–33 again. What does this text tell us about the wife's role in marriage? What does it tell us about the husband's role? In your opinion, which role is more difficult?

4. How does marriage preach the gospel? What does God want it to say about the gospel? Who is listening to that preaching?

5. What does it mean to be humble? How does humility in a parent attract children to that parent and his or her values?

6. What does it mean to be proud? Why does hypocrisy follow pride? Why do proud and hypocritical parents alienate children?

7. In what ways does your marriage teach the gospel? In what ways does your marriage contradict the gospel? In light of this chapter, what does repentance look like?

7

GOSPEL FATHERS

CHRISTIANITY is a patriarchal religion. That means that it is father centered. But patriarchy is in steep decline. According to a recent report, for every male attending an evangelical church in North America, there are two females. The ratio is one to four in the African-American church.[1] If this trend is left unreversed, the church as we know it will not survive. When men abandon church and home, it is a sign that the wheels have come off. That is because male servant leaders energize the Christian church and family.

But the contemporary secular worldview is increasingly matriarchal, and matriarchy has invaded the church. It is doing much mischief. Did you know that women buy most books on parenting? I suggested a book on fatherhood to a publisher. He responded, "Bill, books on fatherhood don't sell. Our studies show that 80 percent of books on parenting are purchased by mothers. They read them and give them to their husbands, but their husbands seldom read them. It is difficult to market fatherhood to a female audience."

According to George Gilder, when women lead church and family, men abdicate.[2] My wife and I attended a two-hundred-year-old African Methodist Episcopal Church. There was much joy, singing, and clapping. (The rhythm was infectious.) The minister was a large, cheerful, middle-aged woman. As the service progressed, I looked around the room. About three-fourths of those in attendance were women. Conspicuously, there were no males between the ages of seventeen and sixty.

This should not have surprised us. When women lead,[3] men withdraw from both church and home. But when male servant-leaders abound, young men eagerly volunteer to serve. Vibrant, godly, male leadership attracts men. It encourages their involvement. It motivates them to serve in church and home. Men are irresistibly attracted to other men who model biblical masculinity.

I have said all of this because this book is about parenting. When men abdicate, their children suffer.[4] When men assume their proper role, parenting thrives. The point of this chapter is that understanding and applying the gospel motivates and trains fathers to be effective parents.

FATHERS ARE GOD'S CHIEF PARENTS

Throughout Scripture, fathers are *the* parents, and their wives are their assistants. The wife is a crucial assistant. Parenting is a team sport. It is very hard to do alone. But in a two-parent family, Dad is the chief parent, the one accountable to God for his family. Mom is there to assist him.

Western culture used to assume this arrangement. Before 1830, virtually every manual on parenting was addressed to fathers.[5] Nancy Gibbs, writing in *Time* magazine, notes, "From the Reformation until the 1830's most parenting manuals were written for fathers. Before this time, society assumed that mothers were assistant fathers. Now it is assumed that fathers are assistant mothers."[6]

Why did previous generations assume the father's lead role? Because culture assumed that the Bible was the primary instruction manual for parents, and the Bible addressed its parenting instructions not to mothers, but to fathers! The unstated assumption in the modern evangelical church is the opposite: Mom is the chief parent, and Dad is her assistant.

Scripture is all about fathers and their children. Genesis recounts the story of Noah and his three sons. Then it tells us about Abraham and his son Isaac, Isaac and his son Jacob, and Jacob and his twelve sons. Their mothers play a background role. Throughout the Old Testament, this pattern remains. Stories about mothers and their children are rare exceptions. Patriarchy was Israel's strength. It is one explanation for the incredible persistence of Judaism over the centuries.

In addition, God holds fathers responsible. Eli, not his wife, was responsible for his failure to adequately parent Hophni and Phinehas. Israel asked for a king because Samuel failed to father his sons (1 Sam. 8:1–9). Solomon ended his life an inveterate womanizer. But David, not Bathsheba, was responsible.

Chapter 2 noted that the Bible contains few direct instructions to parents. Those few God addresses to fathers. For example, Deuteronomy 6:4–7 says,

Hear, O Israel: The LORD our God, the LORD is one. You shall love the LORD your God with all your heart and with all your soul and with all your might. And these words that I command you today shall be on your heart. *You shall teach them diligently to your children,* and shall talk of them when you sit in your house, and when you walk by the way, and when you lie down, and when you rise.

Although God holds fathers responsible to teach and train their children, he holds children responsible to honor *both* parents, but the command is always in the context of the father's overarching authority. "Honor your father *and your mother*, as the LORD your God commanded you, that your days may be long, and that it may go well with you in the land" (Deut. 5:16). Solomon took up the same warning: "Hear, my son, your father's instruction, and forsake not your *mother's teaching*" (Prov. 1:8; see also 6:20).

Mothers also have a crucial role. Fathers delegate to them much of the daily grind of practical parenting, especially in the early years. So Solomon warns, "A wise son makes a glad father, but a foolish son is a sorrow to his mother" (Prov. 10:1); "A wise son makes a glad father, but a foolish man despises his mother" (Prov. 15:20); "The rod and reproof give wisdom, but a child left to himself brings shame to his mother" (Prov. 29:15). The idea latent in these passages is that Mom is Dad's assistant. If she fails to carry out his instruction, she will suffer the fruit in her children.

As we have already seen, there are only two verses instructing parents in the New Testament, and Paul addresses them both to fathers: "Fathers, do not provoke your children to anger, but bring them up in the discipline and instruction of the Lord" (Eph. 6:4); "Fathers, do not provoke your children, lest they become discouraged" (Col. 3:21).

These texts do not deny the crucial role of mothers. Rather, God has designed these texts to encourage fathers to assume their God-given responsibility.

A PRACTICAL EXAMPLE

God holds fathers accountable for parenting because he has given them inordinate influence over their children. The Bible presumes, in the language of the Puritans, that fathers are a mirror in which their children look to put on their spiritual dress.

The June 2003 issue of *Touchstone* magazine published the conclusions of a Swiss study that confirm this proposition. It examined the connection between a parent's church attendance and the future likelihood that his or her children would also attend church. The conclusion? The father's spiritual example was the primary tool that shaped his children's desire to embrace his religion. The mother's spiritual commitments were less decisive.[7]

In this study, when both father and mother attended church regularly, 33 percent of their children ended up as regular churchgoers. But when the father was nonpracticing, and the mother a regular church attender, only 2 percent of their children became regular worshipers. If the father was a regular church attender, but the mother an irregular or nonpracticing church attender, extraordinarily, the percentage of children who became adult church attenders went *up* from 33 percent to 38 percent (with the irregular mother) and 44 percent (with the nonpracticing mother). It was as if loyalty to the father's commitment grew in proportion to Mom's laxity, indifference, or hostility to her husband's religion.

Fig. 4. Influence of parents' church attendance on children

Father's Attendance	Mother's Attendance	Children's Attendance
Regular	Regular	33%
Non-Practicing	Regular	2%
Regular	Irregular	38%
Regular	Non-Practicing	44%
Irregular	Non-Practicing	25%

When a father attended church irregularly and his wife was nonpracticing, 25 percent of their children still became regular church attenders. The study went on to note that this was *twelve times* the yield as when the roles were reversed.

"In short," the study concluded, "if a father does not go to church, no matter how faithful his wife's devotions, only one child in fifty (2%) will probably become regular adult worshippers. If a father goes regularly, regardless of the practice of the mother, between two-thirds and three-quarters of their children will become churchgoers (regular and irregular). If a father goes but irregularly to church, regardless of his wife's devotion, between a half and two-thirds of their offspring will find themselves coming to church regularly or occasionally."

Touchstone continues, "The results are shocking, but they should not be surprising. They are about as politically incorrect as it is possible to be; but they simply confirm what psychologists, criminologists, educationalists, and traditional Christians know. You cannot buck the biology of the created order. Father's influence, from the determination of a child's sex by the implantation of his seed to the funerary rites surrounding his passing, is out of all proportion to his allotted, and severely diminished role, in Western liberal society."

In terms of intimacy, care, and nurture—crucial functions—Mom's role is primary. But it is equally true that when a child begins to move into that period of differentiation from home and engagement with the world "out there," he or she looks increasingly to the father for direction. If the father is indifferent, or just plain absent, that task of differentiation and engagement is much harder. When children see that church is a "women and children" thing, they respond accordingly. They do not go to church, or they attend but their hearts are not in it.[8]

The bottom line is this: We have seen that you cannot feminize the church and keep the men, and you cannot keep the children if you do not keep the men. Here is the formula: When the father is absent or passive, the family withers, and the ability to pass the baton of faith to the next generation is greatly weakened. This does not mean that parenting is hopeless for single parents. God is a father to the fatherless.[9] Timothy was raised by his mother and grandmother, and yet he was a great leader in the early church. Rather, it means that father-centered families are the norm. It means that winning and keeping men is essential to the local Christian church. It means that fatherhood is vital to parenting, and therefore to the salvation of our children.

The social statistics graphically confirm this conclusion. According to Dr. Urie Bronfenbrenner of Cornell University,

Children growing up in father absent households are at a greater risk for experiencing a variety of behavioral and educational problems, including extremes of hyperactivity and withdrawal; lack of attentiveness in the classroom; difficulty in deferring gratification; impaired academic achievement; school misbehavior; absenteeism; involvement in socially alienated peer groups, and the so-called "teenage syndrome" of behaviors that tend to hang together—smoking, drinking, early and frequent sexual experience, and in the more extreme cases, drugs, suicide, vandalism, violence, and criminal acts.[10]

Building on these statistics, the *Fatherhood Initiative* notes: "Teens from fatherless homes are: 5 times more likely to commit suicide, 32 times more likely to run away, 20 times more likely to have behavioral disorders, 14 times more likely to commit rape, 9 times more likely to drop out of high school, 10 times more likely to abuse chemical substances, 9 times more likely to end up in a state-operated institution, and 20 times more likely to end up in prison."[11]

Chapter 2 made the point that Christians parent with eternity in view! Here is the tragedy: The statistics above cite only the temporal maladies that follow the absent or passive father. The spiritual dimensions are much more alarming. As we just saw from the Swiss study, the implications are often eternal.

It is also interesting to note that in the event of a father's death, these statistics do not bear out.[12] Even though the children grow up without a father, they seem to understand that his absence was outside his control, and the children compensate emotionally.

How did all of this happen? According to Dr. David Lyle Jeffrey of Baylor University, it is a rebellion against patriarchal authority: "The downgrading of fatherhood is not just a product of a handful of mediocre sitcoms; it is a significant cultural pattern that can be traced back many years to serious literature.... We see fathers as symbols of responsibility and authority—much the same way that we see God. The rebellion against fatherhood is part of a general rebellion against authority and God, and a step toward narcissism."[13] In modern times, that journey began with the 1960s rebellion against authority. Our children are reaping the bitter harvest of that rebellion.

In summary, God is a patriarch. The Bible is a patriarchal book. God seeks to replicate himself in male servant-leaders. The proclamation of the gospel is a key to the development of male servant leaders.

ATTRACTING MEN

What can we do to attract men to our churches, to excite men about fatherhood? We can do three things. First, we can emphasize objective truth. Men are most apt to respond to the hard edges of the gospel discussed in chapters 3 and 4. Second, we need to develop masculine role models. Men learn masculinity from other men. Third, we should encourage women to promote biblical masculinity.

Fig. 5. Masculine versus feminine mind

Masculine Mind	Feminine Mind
Truth/Facts	Feeling/Emotion
Risk	Caution
Competition	Cooperation
Aggressive	Passive

Men Respond to Objective Truth

In her book *The Feminization of American Culture,* Ann Douglas notes that the theology of Jonathan Edwards (1703–58) was the high-water mark of patriarchy in American culture. She locates its center in the substitutionary atonement preached by Edwards and his disciple Joseph Bellamy (1719–90).[14] Douglas prefers the "softer" feminine model that emerged from the New England Unitarians after Edwards's death. Unitarianism eliminated the objective rigors of the substitutionary atonement (which is the biblical gospel). Unitarians replaced it with a new gospel.[15] H. Richard Niebuhr described it this way: "A God without wrath brought men without sin into a kingdom without judgment through the ministrations of a Christ without a Cross."[16]

Historian Stephen Nichols agrees. He notes how William Ellery Channing (1780–1842), distressed with Puritan doctrine and its transcendent Savior, one who seemed holy and unapproachable, taught a strictly human savior that was intimate, near, affectionate, and easy to approach.[17] Channing spearheaded the transformation of Edwards's New England theology into nineteenth-century Unitarianism. Douglas saw Channing's change as the beginning of the feminization of American culture.

Douglas is on to something. Men respond best to objective truth. By contrast, feeling and sentiment are more apt to appeal to the feminine nature.[18] A recent *New York Times* article confirms these differences. "When men and women take personality tests," notes John Tierney, "some of the old Mars-Venus stereotypes keep reappearing. On average, women are more cooperative, nurturing, cautious and emotionally responsive. Men tend to be more competitive, assertive, reckless and emotionally flat. Clear differences appear in early childhood and never disappear."[19] Tragically, the article went on to suggest that these differences were a problem to be fixed rather than differences to be celebrated.

The biblical gospel is about objective truth, promoted by Edwards and the Puritans, with its hard edges and sharp corners. Chapters 4 and 5 described it, and the masculine mind relates to it. Churches not centered in this biblical gospel, either because the fear of man controls them or because they can't hold conflicting ideas in tension, often lose their masculine membership.

A recent article reported distressing trends in liberal Christian denominations, organizations whose message increasingly appeals to the feminine mind noted by Douglas,

> The number of ordained clergy in . . . the Evangelical Lutheran Church in America—fell from 13,841 in 1990 to 10,493 in 2007. Membership dropped from 5.24 million to 4.77 million during the same time.
>
> In the Presbyterian Church (U.S.A.), the number of ordained clergy serving as pastors dropped from 10,308 in 1990 to 8,705 in 2006. The denomination's membership declined from 2.85 million to 2.26 million during the same time.
>
> The number of Catholic priests in the United States dropped from 35,925 to 27,971 between 1965 and 2007. This occurred despite the fact that, during the same period, the number of U.S. Catholics increased from 45.6 million to 64.4 million.[20]

Although Catholicism's numbers increased by about 50 percent, its male clergy decreased by about 25 percent.

I recently attended a pastors' conference called *Together for the Gospel*. It presents a sharp contrast to these figures. The conference emphasized the objective facts promoted by Edwards and his peers—the substitutionary penal atonement, the holiness of God, the reality of God's wrath, the impossibility of forgiveness without atonement, the exclusivity of Christianity, and the sinfulness of man. Five thousand men attended, most of them young. Approximately 75 percent were under the age of forty.

The lesson? One important way to attract men is to preach the objective truth of the gospel (if you are a pastor). If you are not a pastor, take your family to a church that preaches this message.

Men Learn Masculinity from Masculine Men

If you want to attract and build men, you must find, attract, and build male role models. In his book *Why Men Hate Going to Church*, David Murrow notes,

> You cannot have a thriving church without a core of men who are true followers of Christ. If men are dead, the church is dead. . . .
>
> If we want to change the world, we must focus on men. . . .
>
> When men are absent and anemic the body withers. . . .
>
> The church and the Titanic have something in common: It's women and children first. The great majority of ministry in Protestant churches is focused on children, next on women. . . .

> Men don't follow programs; they follow men. A woman may
> choose a church because of the programs it offers, but a man
> is looking for another man he can follow.[21]

Murrow is right. Men don't follow programs; they follow men.
We are not talking about "macho" behavior. Machismo is a per-
version of biblical masculinity. In fact, it usually occurs because
men feel insecure about their masculinity.

Men are not born masculine. It is learned behavior. Men
are born male. That means they enter the world with a man's
body parts. You can be male and be feminine. You can be a
woman and be masculine. True masculinity expresses itself
as a desire to serve women and children by leading them,
protecting them, and providing for them. True masculinity
is all about unselfish servanthood. It has nothing to do with
muscle size or athletic ability.

Ultimately, men learn masculinity from God. God is not
male. He does not have a body. But God is pure, unadulter-
ated masculinity. Ultimately, he alone is the Christian father's
role model. His masculinity expresses itself as the willingness
to initiate.

A homosexual Buddhist friend once asked why I always
referred to God as *him.* Quoting C. S. Lewis, I cautiously replied,
"God is so masculine that, by contrast, everything that he has
created is feminine."[22] Lewis suggested that the willingness
to initiate is the heart and soul of God's masculinity. God
serves us by initiating. He initiated creation. He initiated our
redemption. He came to us in the incarnation. We didn't go
to him. This willingness is most likely what God means when
he refers to himself with masculine pronouns. Although God

does not have a male body, he is the ultimate initiator. He is the ultimate servant-leader. In this sense, God the Father is absolute masculinity.

By contrast, femininity responds to male initiation. For this reason God calls the church, both male and female, the bride of Christ. God initiated our creation, and he initiated our redemption. And he initiated the relationship that you and I have with him. In our relationship with God, we are all responders. In contrast with God, we are all feminine.

Here is the point: Men learn their masculinity from God. The presence of the living God makes men more masculine and women more feminine.

Jesus Christ models biblical masculinity. The gospel is all about his masculine initiation. First, he initiated our salvation at the cost of his life. He came and sought us out. Then he returned to heaven and sent his Holy Spirit to lead us to the Father. Second, he was a servant-leader of the first order. He leads the church by serving us, and he serves us by leading. Third, he provides for our daily material needs. Fourth, he protects his church at the cost of his life. "While I was with them, I kept them in your name, which you have given me. I have guarded them, and not one of them has been lost except the son of destruction, that the Scripture might be fulfilled" (John 17:12). The deeper a man's relationship with God's Son, the more potent his masculinity will gradually become.

Biblical masculinity doesn't stop there. Men learn it from other men who have been impacted by Christ. Boys learn masculinity from their fathers. "Researchers have determined," writes Jim Dobson in *Time* magazine, "that boys are not born with an understanding of 'maleness.' They have to learn it, ideally from their fathers."[23] In fact, numerous studies have shown that both girls and boys obtain their sexual identity by interaction with their fathers, not their mothers.[24]

"Fathers must train their sons to be masculine and their daughters to be feminine," notes David Wegener. "They must inculcate bravery and initiating, sacrificial love in their sons by teaching, example and practice. Fathers must train their daughters to be nurturers and to respond to the initiating love of a strong and worthy man. They can do this by encouragement and direction and by their own relationship with their daughter."[25]

What I am saying is that first the objective contours of the gospel attract men, then its substance nourishes and stimulates biblical masculinity. As men behold Christ, they are transformed into his image (2 Cor. 3:18). For men, it is the "image" and "likeness" of godly masculinity (Gen. 1:26). Christian men see Jesus dying for his church, and they want to die for their wives and children. They see Jesus leading as a servant, and they want to serve their families by leading. All of this is at the heart of the gospel discussed in chapters 4 and 5.

Fatherhood is on the endangered-species list. The gospel is slowly disappearing from the church, and fatherhood with it. Fatherless families are increasingly the norm. "In the US, in 1960 there were 10 million fatherless homes," reported Dr. Wade Horn. "By 2003, this figure had climbed to 25 million. One in three families is now fatherless."[26] The implications of this fact for the future are cataclysmic for church and family. The gospel is the solution!

Biblical Femininity Encourages Biblical Masculinity

Just as big muscles and athletic ability do not evidence biblical masculinity, so weakness, passivity, and fear do not evidence biblical femininity. Both are caricatures. "Masculinity . . . is a matter of the mind," notes Stuart Scott. "A man can go to the gym to work out and even gain the physique of Charles Atlas or Arnold Schwarzenegger, but this will not make him more masculine. . . . What tells ultimately is, not what is without a man, but what is within."[27]

In the same way, biblical femininity is a constellation of heart qualities. A woman with biblical femininity is strong, convinced, and unshakable. Faith is her bedrock. "Strength and dignity are her clothing, and she laughs at the time to come" (Prov. 31:25). Just as men become more masculine around men who are humble servant leaders, so they become more masculine in the presence of biblical femininity.

Women have great power over men. Men need them desperately. The wise woman leverages this power to encourage biblical masculinity. The first way she can do this is by directing the children to their father. When our children came to Judy with questions, being very competent, she usually knew how to answer, but wanting to involve me, she would often say, "Let's go ask your father." This accomplished two things. First, her behavior honored me in our children's eyes (despite the fact that I often did not deserve it). It also honored the office of fatherhood. Second, it forced me to get involved and assume my God-given responsibilities.

A woman can also encourage masculinity by respecting her husband, especially in front of her children. In the great passage on marriage (Ephesians 5), wives are commanded to do two things: submit to their husbands and respect them. Paul knows that men feel loved when they feel respected. My wife habitually respected me in front of our children, even when I did not earn or deserve it. She did this for the sake of our children. Her faith always humbled me. It caused me to return her respect, knowing that she gave it to me because of her confidence in God's desire to work through her children's father.

Women can also encourage biblical masculinity by praying for it. Ask God to make the men in your life masculine as defined by Christ's example.

Finally, biblical femininity encourages husbands to lead. Effective moms don't nag their husbands; they encourage them. There is a big difference. They encourage men by calling attention to evidences of grace at work in their husbands, not by tearing them down.

Biblical femininity works at making men feel needed. In his classic book *Men and Marriage,* George Gilder points out that men bring only three unique contributions to marriage—leadership, financial provision, and protection.[28] When women assume these roles, men have nothing to contribute, they feel unneeded, and they abdicate. Women who surrender these responsibilities to their husbands infuse them with purpose, and husbands generally respond positively. By surrendering these responsibilities, women encourage biblical masculinity.

SUMMARY

This chapter has suggested that the chief parent in God's economy is the father. His wife is his assistant. The Bible addresses all its verses on parenting to fathers. That is because

God has given each father inordinate power over his children's hearts, and ultimately their spiritual destiny. The general principle holds: As the father goes, so goes the family, and so goes parenting.

Although men are born male, biblical masculinity is learned. We live in a confused age. Both biblical masculinity and femininity are scarce. For the sake of our children, and the glory of God, it is crucial that we rebuild them. How can we do this?

Emphasize the objective truth of the gospel. The male mind responds to it. The gospel has another advantage. It models biblical masculinity for men. It displays God's Son, the only truly masculine man, for our imitation. The gospel displays the potent masculinity of his Father.

Men also learn masculinity from other men who have been impacted by the gospel. Boys unconsciously absorb it from their fathers. Women become increasingly feminine around biblical masculinity, and biblical femininity completes the circle by encouraging masculine behavior.

The gospel attracts men. The gospel teaches men what it means to be masculine. This doesn't work if our gospel is just "Jesus loves you." Gospel-centered churches are factories of biblical masculinity, and biblical parenting thrives in this environment.

STUDY QUESTIONS

1. List as many biblical texts on parenting addressed to moms as you can find.

2. This chapter has suggested that the father's faith and spiritual involvement affects children more than the mother's. Do you think this is true? Why or why not?

3. In your opinion, why do moms buy most books on parenting?

4. In your family, who is the chief parent and who is the assistant?

5. This chapter suggested three things we can do to attract men and encourage biblical masculinity. Which was most important to you? Why?

6. What can leaders in the church do to encourage biblical masculinity?

7. What can wives and moms do to encourage true masculinity in their husbands and sons?

8

FOUNDATIONS OF DISCIPLINE

THE PREVIOUS CHAPTER addressed the importance of patriarchy. The Bible addresses its parenting commands to fathers, not mothers. "Fathers, do not provoke your children to anger, but bring them up in the discipline and instruction of the Lord" (Eph. 6:4). This chapter is about the discipline of the Lord.

Biblical discipline always expresses God's love. "The Lord disciplines the one he *loves*, and chastises every son whom he receives" (Heb. 12:6, quoting Prov. 3:12). Since this is true, Christian parents should discipline. They should imitate God the Father, but like God the Father, their motive should always be love. In fact, the Bible so closely allies discipline with love that it suggests that those who refuse to discipline their children actually hate them: "Whoever spares the rod hates his son, but he who loves him is diligent to discipline him" (Prov. 13:24).

The gospel should be at the heart of all attempts to discipline children. The gospel affects discipline in two ways. First, it motivates our discipline. Second, communicating the gospel becomes the *end* of effective Christian discipline.

Effective discipline requires great resolve and perseverance. No parent is equal to this task. Some children require five spankings in a lifetime, others five every morning.

When my eldest son, David, was about five, he became fascinated with my electric razor. For Dave, the term *strong-willed* was inadequate. When he wanted something, his tenacity was simply astounding. His motives were base. He would weigh the pain of a spanking against what he wanted. If the pain was worth it, he would disobey.

On this particular day, my razor was worth it. He took it down, plugged it in, and turned it on. He knew it was against the rules. The first time I caught him, I spanked him. A few minutes later he turned the razor on again. I was amazed. My spankings hurt. Even today my grown children remember and wince. So I spanked him again. One Sunday afternoon we repeated this routine seven times. I put him to bed exhausted, frustrated, and discouraged, but for David's sake I was determined to win the battle. And a battle it was.

Some would have solved Dave's problem by putting the razor out of reach. Believe me, I gave this serious thought. It would have been the easy way out, but hiding the razor did not address his self-will problem. It just deferred the conflict to another day. So, like most effective field generals, I picked the time and place of battle. Little did I realize the strength of Dave's determination. At least twice I came to the place where I could not control him with spankings. In desperation I went to the elders in my church for prayer. Both times he immediately improved.

Strength of will is a gift from God. The more a child has, the harder it is to break. But be encouraged. Don't give up. Once his or her self-will is broken, this child is more apt to resist peer pressure, lead others, and consistently practice the spiritual disciplines. You will need encouragement. The strong-willed child requires tremendous perseverance and determination. Today, David is deeply committed to Christ. He is a leader of men. In fact, he is a pastor. By God's grace I won the battle, and I am glad I did.

Understanding the gospel and its implications for disciplining our children fortified Judy and me through these trials. It helped in several ways:

- The gospel convinced us that indwelling sin was our children's problem.
- The gospel convinced us that authority is a crucial parental issue.
- The gospel instructed us to pursue our children's hearts rather than their behavior.
- The gospel motivated us to use discipline to preach the gospel to our children.
- The gospel motivated us to fear God.
- The gospel helped Judy and me to grow in humility and sincerity.

INDWELLING SIN

Before we can apply an appropriate solution, we must first diagnose the problem. If my car won't start because the gas tank is empty, a trip to the gas station is the solution. But if the starter motor is defective, I need an appointment with the repair shop. In the same way, addressing problems with our children starts with a correct diagnosis.

So what is your child's basic problem? Why does he lie, cheat, and steal? Why does she bite her sister? Why are your children restless, selfish, or angry? Why do they talk back to their parents? If the problem is disease, if they are sick, medication is the answer. They are not morally responsible. If the problem is the child's environment, a change of surroundings is the answer. But if the problem is a fallen nature (indwelling sin), then discipline and instruction are the only effective solutions.

Most secular diagnoses are faulty because they assume the child is basically good. My eldest daughter has a bachelor's degree in early childhood development. The one fact that her professors consistently pounded home was the conviction that children are basically good. If that is your assumption, the root of your child's misbehavior must be a disease or a defective environment. That is why many rebellious, self-willed children are now diagnosed with ODD, Oppositional Defiant Disorder. Web MD lists some of its symptoms—temper tantrums, arguing with adults, refusing to abide by rules, blaming others for one's mistakes, outbursts of anger, and so on. Web MD claims that the cause is biology, genetics, or environment. (Sin is not even on the horizon.) A pediatrician told me that some parents pay for MRIs on their children's brains, looking for symptoms of ODD. Since the problem is physical, not moral, the solution is not discipline or instruction. It is psychotherapy or medication.

Others blame the child's environment. The teacher is not supportive. His classmates are not friendly. Her neighborhood friends are a bad example. She watches too much TV. If only he didn't play computer games eight hours a day. If a bad environment is the diagnosis, then a change of surroundings is the solution.

The Bible presents a different diagnosis. Your child's behavior is a symptom of what Scripture calls the flesh—that is, indwelling sin manifesting itself as pride and selfishness.

If the problem is spiritual and moral, then the solution is the discipline and instruction of the Lord. Although Christians recognize that their children can have physical problems such as hyperactivity and that their children's environment can also affect them, the fundamental diagnosis is more simple and straightforward. Temper tantrums, arguing, and failure to accept correction are the result of plain old-fashioned sin. "Christians should be slow to 'medicalize' problems the Bible calls sin," notes Dr. Timothy Sisemore.[1]

As one faithful parent always reminds me, "The heart of the problem is a problem heart." They act bad because they are bad. Our children are radically disordered at the deepest and most basic level. "The heart is deceitful above all things, and desperately sick; who can understand it?" (Jer. 17:9). Here is how God sees your child: "None is righteous, no, not one; no one understands; no one seeks for God" (Rom. 3:10–11, quoting Ps. 14:1, 3). Therefore, they are "by nature children of wrath, like the rest of mankind" (Eph. 2:3). What the thera-peutic community often calls ADD or ODD the Bible simply labels "works of the flesh": "Now the works of the flesh are evident: sexual immorality, impurity, sensuality, idolatry, sor-cery, enmity, strife, jealousy, fits of anger, rivalries, dissensions, divisions, envy, drunkenness, orgies, and things like these" (Gal. 5:19–21).

If heart corruption is the diagnosis, a pill or change of environment will not solve the problem. Such things may temporarily suppress symptoms, but they won't address the underlying issue. The short-term solution is the "discipline and instruction of the Lord" (Eph. 6:4). "Folly is bound up in the heart of a child, but the rod of discipline drives it far from him" (Prov. 22:15).

The long-term solution is more radical. It is the heart trans-plant that occurs at new birth. "A *new heart*, and a new spirit I will put within you," promises Ezekiel. "And I will remove the heart of stone from your flesh and *give you a heart of flesh*. And I will put my Spirit within you, and cause you to walk in my statutes and be careful to obey my rules" (Ezek. 36:26–27).

In all of this a clear grasp of the gospel is crucial. The gospel convinces us that our children have a heart problem. It convinces us that it is systemic. That means that it is woven deeply into every strand of our nature. You can't chop off a bad limb and get rid of it. The problem infiltrates every aspect of our being. Your children inherited the problem from you, their parent.

The gospel lets us see their sin through God's eyes. It con-fronts us. We see how serious the heart problem really is. Even if your child had done nothing wrong, Christ would still have had to die for that child. That is because their *nature* is the problem. The singular word *sin* is Paul's term for our fallen nature. Jesus had to atone for our nature (sin, who we are) before he could atone for our sins (what we do). Notice the language in Romans 8:3. God sent his "own Son in the likeness of sinful flesh and for *sin*, he condemned *sin* in the flesh." This means that your child's *nature* is so seriously corrupted that it required a substitute's slow death by excruciating torture to atone for it. Again, this would have been necessary even if your child had never actually done anything wrong.

Most evangelical parents do not share this conviction, and this breakdown is responsible for many parenting failures. A friend remarked to his father, a faithful evangelical for over thirty five years, that his children needed regular spankings because their hearts were inclined toward evil. Shocked, his father answered, "They are not sinners. Children are innocent. They are not accountable to God until the age of accountability. Your pessimism concerns me."

This response articulates an ancient heresy called *Pelagianism*. Pelagianism is the idea that we are born innocent, that our natures are essentially good, that God does not consider us sinners until we do something wrong. As R. C. Sproul observes, the acceptance of this belief is widespread,

> In a George Barna poll, more than seventy percent of "professing evangelical Christians" in America expressed the belief that man is basically good. And more than eighty percent articulated the view that God helps those who help themselves. These positions . . . are both Pelagian. To say that we're basically good is the Pelagian view. . . . We're overwhelmed with it. We're surrounded by it. We're immersed in

it. We hear it every day. We hear it every day in the secular culture. And not only do we hear it every day in the secular culture, we hear it every day on Christian television and on Christian radio.[2]

But our children are not basically good, and the proof that the heart of the problem is a problem heart should be obvious to any observant parent, even those who don't believe in the Bible. For example, you don't need to teach your children to be bad. Bad behavior comes naturally. "I remember this hitting me years ago as a kindergarten teacher," writes Paul David Tripp. "I never had to teach my children to hit one another, to be jealous, to speak unkindly, to push to the front of the line, to announce that their lunch was better than their neighbor's, to brag about their achievements, and to turn everything into a competition."[3]

The real world is the opposite. You must teach your children to be good—and if you don't, they won't be. Good behavior doesn't come naturally. If good behavior came naturally, but we had to teach our children to be bad, we could make a case for Pelagianism. But that is not how it works. Children learn good behavior only through the sweaty persistence of their parents. Any parent who has stood between a two-year-old and the cookie jar knows this. The first word your child learns is not *yes* ("Yes, Mommy. How can I serve you?"). It is *no*. Your two-year-old does not have to be taught to turn around and go the other way when called. It is natural—as are temper tantrums, disrespectful speech, and pouting.

For these reasons, Pelagianism is behind most parental failure. If you have not correctly diagnosed the problem, you will not apply the proper solution. God has made the diagnosis. From the moment of birth, our children are inclined toward evil from the heart out. He has given us the solution to the majority of our children's behavioral issues: "Do not withhold discipline from a child; if you strike him with a rod, he will not die" (Prov. 23:13); "The rod and reproof give wisdom, but a child left to himself brings shame to his mother" (Prov. 29:15).

Not only does the gospel convince us that sin is the problem, it also imparts to us a sense of urgency. The cross proclaims God's infinite passion for justice. It reminds us that someday our children will get perfect justice. There will be no exceptions. That means that our children enter the world in trouble, and that is why Jesus took their place on the cross. He died to satisfy the demands of God's perfect justice in their place. The implication is clear. Either our children will satisfy God's justice by suffering something akin to crucifixion in hell for eternity (that is what our sins deserve), or they will believe and let Jesus satisfy God's justice in their place. One of these fates awaits each of our children. Parents who believe this feel a tremendous sense of urgency. The stakes are high.

The gospel also gives us a window on how God feels about sin. He hates it. It provokes his wrath. At the cross we see how God feels about our child's complaining, rebellion, temper tantrums, selfishness, and lack of self-control. The cross says, "God hates these heart attitudes. They deserve crucifixion." This is an unpopular idea. Yet, if true, how can we be passive about our children's heart sins and claim to love them?

For this reason, those clear on the gospel practice corporal discipline—appropriate spanking at an appropriate age. The world says, "Corporal punishment is child abuse." But the Bible answers, "*Failure* to discipline is child abuse."

Physical abuse of children does occur, and Christians abhor it. But it usually occurs when there is a disconnect between corporal punishment and loving, stable, two-parent families. Social studies[4] show that behind most opposition to spanking is a social worker's experience with an angry, abusing stepfather or live-in boyfriend. Where these natural bonds of love and affection do not exist, temptations to abuse abound. But that is not biblical discipline.

In summary, the gospel convinces both parent and child that sin—deep, systemic heart disfigurement—is our child's fundamental problem. For this Jesus died. He also died for the sins that these hearts produce. The cross gives us a window into God's hatred of evil, and what awaits the child not led into saving faith through the loving discipline and instruction of his or her parents. The gospel solution is corporal punishment applied by loving, committed parents. The cross motivates consistent, godly discipline.

BELIEVE IN AUTHORITY

To discipline effectively, not only must Christian parents understand sin, they must also have a deep conviction about the goodness and appropriateness of authority. "For many in our culture," notes Steve Farrar, "and especially in academia, anything 'authoritative' is bad."[5] Farrar is right. Authority is not popular. It doesn't take a rocket scientist to smell the animosity to authority in Western culture.

After extensive polling of Christian parents, George Barna notes that "many parents suggest that being a 'command and control' type of parent is uncalled for or even counterproductive. They describe such behavior as 'over the top,' 'domineering,' 'insensitive,' 'compensation for personal weakness,' and 'not loving.'" [6] Yet Barna (speaking for many others) goes on to show that strong authority, coupled with affection, is the most effective parenting style. The Bible takes authority seriously and positively.

Effective parents see authority with biblical eyes. God loves authority and hates rebellion.

> [Elisha] went up from there to Bethel, and while he was going up on the way, some small boys came out of the city and jeered at him, saying, "Go up, you baldhead! Go up, you baldhead!" And he turned around, and when he saw them, he cursed them in the name of the LORD. And two she-bears came out of the woods and tore forty-two of the boys. (2 Kings 2:23–24)

This is a strong text. God's response to rebellion against his prophet demonstrates how he feels about mocking authority. All authority is from God (Rom. 13). Therefore, rebellion against lawful authority is rebellion against God himself. Mocking Elisha was mocking God. If this seems extreme, it is probably because you and I see authority differently, through the eyes of contemporary culture.

Other biblical texts that describe God's feelings about child rebellion are similar. "The eye that mocks a father and scorns to obey a mother will be picked out by the ravens of the valley and eaten by the vultures" (Prov. 30:17). This does not mean that the ravens are going to swoop down every time your child rebels. Rather, this text reveals how God *feels* about that rebellion. It tells us what your child's self-will deserves.

Parental authority is most important. Despite your imperfections, and for the sake of your children, God has given you authority. "Let every person be subject to the governing authorities," Paul exhorts. "For there is no authority except from God, and those that exist have been instituted by God. Therefore whoever resists the authorities resists what God has appointed, and those who resist will incur judgment" (Rom. 13:1–2). You are God's "instituted" authority in your child's life. Parents who tolerate child rebellion mock God's authority and expose their little ones to God's "judgment." If you love them, you will teach them to submit to your authority.

Biblical parents don't just exercise authority. They exercise servant-authority. Parents are shepherds of the smallest biblical flock. Therefore, Paul's charge to Timothy applies also to parents. (In fact, pastors learn how to apply this text to the church by first applying it to their children.)

> I charge you in the presence of God and of Christ Jesus, who is to judge the living and the dead, and by his appearing and his kingdom: preach the word; be ready in season and out of season; reprove, rebuke, and exhort, with complete patience and teaching. (2 Tim. 4:1–2)

"Preach the word" to your children? Preaching assumes authority. Parenting involves "reprov[ing], rebuk[ing], and exhort[ing], with complete patience and teaching."

Paul's charge to Timothy assumes other truths as well. It assumes a clear diagnosis of your child's problem: sin. It assumes the fear of God, rooted in a clear grasp of eternal realities (chapter 3). It assumes awareness of the judgment to come. Paul reminds Timothy to read these words in the presence of God, who will "judge the living and the dead." That means that we are to discipline our children in the awareness of the truth that someday God will judge both us and our children. Is that truth real to you? To the degree that it is real, you will be an effective disciplinarian.

Where do we gain God's perspective on authority? We obtain it from the gospel. The gospel convinces us that authority matters. The gospel reminds us that God has sewn authority into the warp and woof of the universe—the Trinity, the ultimate reality that has existed from before time began.

The Trinity is the original community. It has always been and always will be. God created humanity to glorify the moral beauty of this primal Society. Here is the point: *The Trinity is inherently authoritative and hierarchical.* Therefore, if Christian culture, including families, is to imitate God, it must be also. Children learn to exercise and submit to servant-authority in their families. Dr. Bruce Ware reminds us that

> We live in a culture that despises authority at every level. . . . We find it hard to think about authority for one simple reason: We are sinners who want to be in charge of our own lives. . . . One of the lessons of the Trinity is that God loves what we despise; namely, God loves, exercises, and embraces rightful authority-submission relationships. God loves this authority-submission structure because God

embodies this very structure in his Trinitarian relations of Persons.[7]

We see trinitarian authority worked out in the gospel. Although the members of the Trinity are equal in value, they relate to each other in an ordered hierarchy, and they delight to have it this way.

The Father exercises servant-authority. His authority is not selfish. It is the authority of the ultimate servant. The Son never commands the Father. Rather, he submits to the Father. The Father commands the Son. The Holy Spirit never commands Father and Son. Rather, he submits to Father and Son. The Son and Spirit do not resent submission. Rather, it is their joy. They love to submit. That is because submission to God's authority is inherently good, virtuous, and beautiful. The Father does not feel superior because he exercises authority. He is a servant. He directs the Son with infinite love. Here is what the Son's submission looks like.

> Have this mind among yourselves, which is yours in Christ Jesus, who, though he was in the form of God, did not count equality with God a thing to be grasped, but made himself nothing, taking the form of a *servant*, being born in the likeness of men. And being found in human form, he *humbled himself* by *becoming obedient* to the point of death, even death on a cross. (Phil. 2:5–8)

Jesus did not cling to his rights. Instead, he "made himself nothing," became a slave, humbled himself, and became obedient to the point of death, even death on a cross. Jesus submitted. He obeyed his Father's authority. Submission to authority expresses humility, and God always exalts the humble. So the Father raised Jesus to his right hand and gave him all power and authority.

God calls the church out of darkness, and into this same marvelous light, to internalize in us, and display through us, the beauty of divine authority. He commands parents to exercise servant-authority as God the Father does. He commands children to joyfully submit to their parents' authority.[8] It is no small issue. Ultimately, life is about authority. At the final judgment, how we responded to God's authority will determine our eternal destiny.

I recently witnessed this exchange: Mom asked her grade-school-aged daughter to help set the table. "Why should I set the table?" the daughter answered resentfully. "I'm tired of doing your work. Set the table yourself. None of my friends have to set the table. Why should I be different?"

How should love respond? It would call this mother to discipline her child in love. Why? The eternal and temporal consequences of this rebellion are deeply disturbing. Someday "every knee [will] bow . . . and every tongue confess that Jesus Christ is Lord" (Phil. 2:10–11). The day will come when we will "go out and look on the dead bodies of the men who have *rebelled against [God]*. For their worm shall not die, their fire shall not be quenched, and they shall be an abhorrence to all flesh" (Isa. 66:24). It is impossible to believe this, love your children, and not discipline them.

SUMMARY

Clarity about sin and authority are the foundations of parental discipline. Our culture aggressively rejects both.

Therefore, we must be clear about sin. Before we can apply the appropriate solution, we must diagnose the problem. Both we and our children suffer from fallen natures. Our hearts are corrupt at the most basic level. Our children's behavioral problems all go back to this fundamental moral and spiritual reality. But there is hope. Appropriate, compassionate corporal discipline is God's gracious solution. When applied with love and affection, it bears wonderful fruit.

We must also be clear about authority. God puts parents in children's lives to exercise loving, gracious authority. When they rebel, your response should be immediate, decisive, age appropriate, determined, loving, gracious, and repeated until you have won the battle. "Whoever spares the rod hates his son, but he who loves him is diligent to discipline him" (Prov. 13:24). "Discipline your son, for there is hope; do not set your heart on putting him to death" (Prov. 19:18). Like Paul I urge you, "In the presence of God and of Christ Jesus, who is to judge the living and the dead, and by his appearing and his kingdom" (2 Tim. 4:1), to exercise servant-uthority in the lives of your children.

STUDY QUESTIONS

1. In your own words, what was this chapter trying to say?

2. Read the following Scriptures: Prov. 3:11–12; 13:24; 19:18, 25; 20:30; 22:15; 23:13–14; 29:15, 19; Eph. 6:4. How does the gospel described in chapters 4 and 5 impact your view of them?

3. What did this chapter mean by the term *indwelling sin?* Can you define what it means to be Pelagian? How does this differ from the conviction that our children are born with indwelling sin? How would Pelagianism affect a parent's approach to parenting?

4. Why is a proper understanding of authority crucial to effective discipline? What does the relationship between the Father and the Son teach us about exercising and submitting to authority?

5. What passages in Scripture let us in on how God feels about rebellion against lawful authority? (Hint: See 1 Sam. 2:27–35; 2 Kings 2:23–25; Prov. 30:17.)

9

DISCIPLINE THAT PREACHES

So far, we have said that effective disciplinarians are clear on the issues of sin and authority. Now we need to discuss the target of that authority. Chapter 1 suggested that the heart is the target. The goal is not just morality. It is new birth. We do not get new birth by being moral; rather, new birth produces biblical morality. Therefore, wise parents aim their discipline at the *heart*. Fundamentally, Christian parents discipline heart attitudes, not behaviors.

AIM FOR THE HEART

To discipline in such a way, we must see our child's heart as God sees it. Paul David Tripp says,

If my heart is the source of my sin problem, then lasting change must always travel through the pathway of my heart. It is not enough to alter my behavior or to change my circumstances. Christ transforms people by radically changing their hearts. If the heart doesn't change, the person's words and behavior may change temporarily because of an external pressure or incentive [the pain of discipline]. But when the pressure or incentive is removed, the changes will disappear.[1]

In other words, if the threat of pain or the promise of reward is the only motivation, my child will perform only in the presence of the threat or promise. But the heart captured by God will increasingly do right even when the prospect is short-term pain.

The heart is the center of our personality. We speak out of our hearts: "For out of the abundance of the heart the mouth speaks" (Matt. 12:34). Shouting, lying, gossip, rudeness, critical speech, complaining, and disrespectful speech all originate in our child's heart: "But what comes out of the mouth proceeds from the heart, and this defiles a person" (Matt. 15:18). We lust from the heart: "Everyone who looks at a woman with lustful intent has already committed adultery with her in his heart" (Matt. 5:28). We worship idols with our hearts (Matt. 6:21). In fact, all sin proceeds from the heart: "For out of the heart come evil thoughts, murder, adultery, sexual immorality, theft, false witness, slander" (Matt. 15:19).

This means that changing external behavior is not the issue. We must get to the heart of the matter, and as we have said, the heart of our child's problem is a problem heart. If we reach the heart, the desired behavior will follow permanently and volitionally.

When my son Joseph was about five, he spilled his milk three times during one meal. I was angry and frustrated; I wanted to discipline him, but I didn't. His heart was in the right place. He was genuinely trying to please us. The spills were caused by immaturity and awkwardness.

Later that evening, however, I asked him to get ready for bed. He pouted, skulked, and moped around the house. Here was a heart issue. His demeanor said, "I'm angry that I must go to bed. I deserve better." This time I spanked him and held him until he quit crying. After he asked God to forgive him, I went for his heart.

"Joseph, what do you really deserve? Do you deserve to stay up late?"

He looked down, ashamed, and didn't answer.

"The gospel reminds us that we all deserve crucifixion. This includes Mom, Dad, and you. Here is the amazing truth: Because God loves you, you are not getting crucifixion. Jesus took it in your place. Instead, tonight you got a hot, nutritious dinner, and now you get to sleep between clean, warm sheets. On top of all that, God gave you parents who love you. Can you agree that God has given you much better than you deserve? Can you be thankful?"

We discussed this subject for some time. By the time I tucked him into bed, he was happy, contented, and very grateful for God's kindness expressed to him through the gospel.

Here is the point: Aim your discipline at your child's heart. I used this discipline event to remind Joseph of the gospel. The Bible says that we are "born again . . . through the living and abiding word of God" (1 Peter 1:23). The gospel is the Word of God. It is "living and abiding." It has great power to change your child. When it does, godly behavior follows.

Had I just spanked Joseph and walked away, I might have retarded future pouting with fear, but I would not have influenced his heart. The gospel impacted his heart and led to long-term change. Eventually, the desired behavior followed. Today Joseph is a grateful, well-adjusted Christian adult.

This approach is even more important in the teen years. (Read *The Age of Opportunity* by Paul David Tripp for excellent instruction on how to go about this.)

USING DISCIPLINE TO TEACH THE GOSPEL

We have seen that the cross informs us about indwelling sin. It motivates us to become authority figures, and it teaches us to aim for our children's hearts. It also motivates us to make each discipline event an occasion to teach, re-explain, and reinforce the gospel. Gospel-centered parents use discipline to help their children see sin through God's eyes, to help them see that heart-sins are the real issue, that sin has consequences, that God forgives us on the basis of his Son's cross, not our performance, and that God disciplines us *because* he loves us.[2]

Here is a suggested model for how to do this. It is not explicitly laid out in Scripture, but the principles can be found in the Bible. Therefore, be careful not to turn it into a legalism.

Let's assume that you ask your six-year-old to come to dinner. She is watching *VeggieTales*. When you ask a second time, she says, "No." How should you respond? You should rejoice. This is a great opportunity to refresh your child's understanding of the gospel.

The first step is the most difficult. It is consistency. Pat Fabrizio reminds us that every time your child rebels and you ignore it, you are training your child. If she throws herself on the floor and you say, "If you don't stop in three minutes, I'm going to discipline you," you are training her that a three-minute temper tantrum is okay. If you say, "I am going to count to five. If you don't respond, I will discipline you," you are training your child to disobey until you count to five.

We are always training. There is no neutrality. When your child knows that disrespectful speech is against the rules, and you say, "If you do that again, I will have to spank you," you are training him that the rules don't matter. He can get away with the first act of rebellion. You are also telling him that rebellion against authority is no big deal.[3] It is much better to stop and spank him without further command. When your child knows the rules, and has broken them, nothing further needs to be said.

God expects us to obey on the first command. It is how we express love for him. "If you love me," Jesus said, "you will keep my commandments" (John 14:15). It is our duty to train our children to express love for God by obeying. That is why it is a great disservice to teach your child to obey on the third or fourth demand. Train your children to respond on the first command.

Second, always put your discipline in the context of love. Say something like this: "The Bible tells us that God disciplines us because he loves us. That is why I discipline you. I love you. Your disrespectful speech, the way you ignored your mother's authority, if left unchecked, will eventually cause you great pain. Most importantly, if I don't discipline you, God will. Because I fear God, and because I love you, I'm going to spank you."

Third, when appropriate, reference Scripture. In this case, you might read James 3:8–9: The tongue "is a restless evil, full of deadly poison. With it we bless our Lord and Father, and with it we curse people who are made in the likeness of God." Take a moment to show your child how Scripture speaks to her sin. Remind her that her heart is the problem. Rebellious speech reveals a rebellious heart. The speech won't change until the heart does. This convinces the child that you are under God's authority, that you are responsible to a higher law, and that she should be also.

Fourth, make sure it hurts. There must be a breaking of the child's self-will. When that occurs, the child will no longer be angry with you, has taken responsibility for his or her action, has sincerely confessed wrongdoing, and is repentant. Making it hurt is difficult for many parents, but children must be controlled. If a parent does not control with spanking, the only other alternative is the verbal abuse of guilt manipulation or accusation. This is infinitely more harmful to a child than loving, careful spanking that hurts.

It must hurt enough to earn the child's fear and respect. I can remember my mother spanking me. It didn't hurt. I was about twelve. But I pretended that it hurt so that she wouldn't actually hurt me. This is not ideal. Instead, you want to discipline with the determination of John Wesley (1703–91), who wrote, "Whatever pains it costs, conquer their stubbornness;

break the will, *if you would not damn the child.* I adjure you not to neglect, not to delay this!"[4]

Fifth, hold the child until he or she stops crying. This communicates love and affection. It connects the pain of discipline with physical affection. This connection will be very important when, in later life, God takes over your child's discipline.

Sixth, as I have already suggested, use the discipline event to rehearse the gospel. Your children cannot hear it too frequently. You don't want them to be among the 70 percent of those attending Christian youth groups, mentioned in chapter 1, who abandon the faith by their early twenties. Your children are proud. They will be tempted to reject the gospel. They will want to be good enough. They won't want to admit that God is holy or that they are sinful and are in trouble.

Seventh, ask them to verbally confess the specific sin for which they are being disciplined. "Are you ready to ask God to forgive you for the sin of rebellious speech?"

If the child answers "no," your discipline has not succeeded. You may need to start over again.

If your precious charge answers "yes," have him or her ask God's forgiveness. Be sure to finish by reminding the child of the grace provided by the gospel. "God is holy. For this one sin you might have gone to hell. But God loves you. He is also infinitely gracious. He does not give us what our sins deserve. His Son was punished on the cross in your place. Because you believe, and no other reason, God now sees you clothed in Jesus' respect for authority. He forgives and accepts you on the basis of that faith alone."

These teaching moments greatly impact children. I remember explaining how Jesus substituted for us on the cross to my eight-year-old daughter, Anne. The next day her brother got in trouble. She came to me and said, "I want to be like Jesus. Can I take David's punishment in his place?"

I explained that it didn't work that way, but I was thrilled that she had clearly understood and internalized the heart of the gospel.

Finally, have your child perform restitution. If the child has harmed someone, he or she needs to make it right. When I found out that my third-grade son, David, had stolen candy from the local pharmacy, we went through the steps mentioned above. The next morning I took him to the pharmacy. David put a dollar on the counter and, in tears, confessed, "I stole a Snickers bar, Mr. Jones, and here is money to repay you."

The pharmacist took the money, looked at David, and also began to cry. Then he looked at me as if to say, "How could you do this to your son?" To say the least, I felt awkward. But I made David perform restitution because I loved him. Dave left with a keen sense of God's justice, God's forgiveness, and the price of sin.

In summary, God the Father is our model. How does he parent? First, he parents us sacrificially. He sent his Son to die so that he could adopt millions of children into his family. The cross is the measure of all parental love. It will need to affect you if you are going to imitate God the Father.

Second, God parents us purposefully. His end is our holiness. Holy children are happy children. Scripture says, "He disciplines us for our good, that we may share his holiness" (Heb. 12:10). You also should parent with a clear idea of what the finished product is to look like.

Third, he disciplines us—painfully, if necessary. He makes it hurt. "For the moment all [of God's] discipline seems *painful* rather than pleasant, but later it yields the peaceful fruit of righteousness to those who have been trained by it" (Heb. 12:11). God does this because he loves us. He has our temporal and eternal happiness in view. The same motive should energize all of our attempts to discipline our children.

THE FEAR OF GOD

Chapter 3 made the point that God blesses the parents who fear him. The fear of God is crucial. It connects us with ultimate reality. The fear of God makes us willing to discipline. The fear of God motivates us to persist in discipline.

The fear of God reminds us that failure to discipline has consequences. If we don't discipline our children, God will. Either we will use the rod on our children, as God commands, or someday God might use our children's miseries (divorce, bankruptcy, inability to hold down a job) as a rod to discipline them *and* even us for our failure to take him seriously. He prefers that we discipline our children. By the time it has become necessary for God to do our job, the day of small pains is past. God's discipline can make the most painful spankings a kindness by comparison. Eli failed to discipline his sons. It cost him his life, the lives of his sons, and the loss of the priesthood (see 1 Sam. 2). Parents who fear God believe that God cares about how we parent, and it motivates them.

Sandy is a young mom who fears God. She asked her toddler to come to her. The child looked at her, turned around, and walked the other way. Sandy knew her daughter had understood, so she picked her up, spanked her, and held her until she finished crying. Then she placed her back in the middle of the room, backed away, and tried again.

"Cathy, please come to me." This time her daughter obeyed.

"That was impressive," I said. "What motivated you?"

"The fear of God," she answered. "I looked at the cross and saw God's verdict about my child's rebellion. To most this sin is a small thing, but I know God doesn't see it that way. My daughter's self-will caused Christ's crucifixion. I thought of the price Jesus paid and then the price my precious daughter would pay if I did not teach her the humility that produces obedience, so I spanked her."

This is an example of how the fear of God impacts parenting. Paul reminds us that holiness is perfected in the fear of God (2 Cor. 7:1). To the degree that we understand the cross, we fear God. We get serious about parenting God's way.

The fear of God has a second benefit. It equips parents to overcome the fear of their children. Tim, a longtime friend, confessed that he did not discipline his three-year-old because he feared his son's disapproval. He was afraid that his son would reject him, resent him, or respond with uncontrollable anger.

The fear of God equips parents to overcome the fear of their children. They can disappoint their children, but they dare not disappoint God. Why? They believe that God is sovereign over their children's hearts. God holds all the strings. He is in control. Those who *really* believe this are free to be God pleasers rather than child fearers. Parents lacking this confidence will often be slaves to their children's approval. Parents who fear God have only one audience: God. If they please him, they are confident that he will produce the results they seek in their children.

SUMMARY

In this chapter and the previous one, we have seen that our conviction about sin shapes our approach to disciplining children. The gospel described in chapters 4 and 5 impacts and shapes our view of sin. It convinces us that our children are sinners.

The gospel speaks to us about authority. God exercises servant-authority and commands us to submit to it with joy. He hates rebellion. He has woven his authority into the very nature of reality. The Trinity, the archetypal community, is hierarchical and authoritative. The gospel expresses that reality. Our parenting should also.

The gospel convinces us that the heart of our children's problem is a problem heart. Therefore, we should aim our discipline at heart attitudes, not behavior.

We have seen that every discipline event is an opportunity to reemphasize and teach the gospel. We suggested seven discipline steps that will constantly reinforce the gospel.

Finally, we have seen how all of this culminates in the fear of God. A parent who fears God will discipline his or her children. The gospel teaches us the fear of God.

Ephesians 6:4 reads, "Fathers, do not provoke your children to anger, but bring them up in the discipline and instruction of the Lord." We have discussed the "discipline of the Lord." The subject of the next chapter is the "instruction of the Lord."

STUDY QUESTIONS

1. If someone asked you what it would look like for parents to aim their discipline at their child's heart, how would you respond? What is the difference between disciplining action and disciplining the heart?

2. Describe the steps suggested in this chapter for turning the discipline event into an opportunity to teach your child the gospel. Practically speaking, in the real world, what hampers your attempts to do this?

3. How should the fear of God affect parents as they approach the important subject of discipline?

10

FOOD FOR THE HUNGRY

EPHESIANS 6:4 READS, "Fathers, do not provoke your children to anger, but bring them up in the discipline and instruction of the Lord." Chapters 8 and 9 discussed the "discipline of the Lord." This chapter tackles the second half of this admonition, "the instruction of the Lord."

One of today's most popular slogans is "You are what you eat." My adult daughters are conscientious mothers. They make a special point of buying organic food for their children. If their children are going to become what they eat, they at least want them to be "organic," not synthetic.

But if you are like me, the slogan has proved true. You have begun to look like your favorite foods—potato chips, tortilla chips, and salsa. One of my friends makes it a practice to eat every day from one of the four basic food groups—salt, sugar, fat, and caffeine. Too often, I have followed his example.

It is the same in the spiritual realm. We become what we eat. Jesus said, "I am the bread of life" (John 6:35). Protein, carbohydrates, and vegetables sustain physical life. If we are fortunate, we will live for sixty to eighty years. But the food that sustains our children for *eternity* is infinitely more important, and Christian parenting is all about that food.

For this reason, God takes the responsibility to feed our children very seriously. Paul writes, "If anyone does not provide for his relatives, and especially for members of his household, he has denied the faith and is *worse than an unbeliever*" (1 Tim. 5:8). In this passage, material food is Paul's concern. The lazy father, the one who doesn't work to earn bread for his children, is "worse than an unbeliever." Strong language! This man has failed a crucial responsibility, and his actions deny the very faith he professes.

If Paul can write so stridently about the failure to provide material food, which nourishes our bodies for only a few short years, what would he say to the father who fails to put the Bread of Life before his children? The gospel is the Bread of Life. The failure of a father to provide material food will be fatal to his children, but if that father fed his children the Bread of Life, even though they died physically, they would still live forever. Failure to feed our children the Bread of Life has catastrophic, eternal consequences. It is an infinitely more serious failure than not providing for material needs.

Your children will become what they eat, both physically and spiritually. That is why it is so important for fathers to set the Bread of Life before their children. What are you feeding them?

Four beliefs or attitudes hinder our willingness to feed our children. First, we believe that we can delegate the job to others and not do it ourselves. Second, we lack confidence in the potency of the Bread of Life—the gospel. Third, we don't have confidence that we can apply the gospel to our children. Fourth, we don't feel competent to teach our children. The purpose of this chapter is to help you conquer these false ideas.

WHO IS THE TEACHER?

Christian parents argue about where they should educate their children—public school, private school, or home school. How does the Bible address this issue? It is silent about where our children should go to school, but it is not silent about who should do the educating. "*Fathers*, do not provoke your children to anger, but bring them up in the discipline and *instruction* of the Lord" (Eph. 6:4). "God has designed your family," notes Voddie Baucham—"not the youth group, not the children's ministry, not the Christian school, but your family—as the principal discipling agent in your children's lives."[1]

Most fathers do not understand the power that God has given them over their children's hearts. George Barna surveyed over a thousand couples who had raised young adults who had a robust faith, and were actively committed to local churches. What was their secret? Although Barna notes that fewer than one in ten Christian families read the Bible *together* at least once a week, these successful parents had routinely conducted family devotions, discussed how to apply the Bible to life's problems, and had formal times of worship and Bible study. Formal family Bible study was a crucial key to their success![2]

I am not suggesting that we return to the *Little House on the Prairie*. Nor do we want fathers to quit their jobs to homeschool their children. But ultimately our expectations about who the chief teacher is should come from the Bible. To fathers, Moses commands,

> These words that I command you today shall be on your heart. *You shall teach them diligently to your children*, and shall talk of them when you sit in your house, and when you walk by the way, and when you lie down, and when you rise. You shall bind them as a sign on your hand, and they shall be as frontlets between your eyes. You shall write them on the doorposts of your house and on your gates. (Deut. 6:6–9)[3]

Notice the priority. First, God's commands are to be upon the *father's* heart. Knowing the gospel is not enough. He needs to feel conviction about it. When is he to teach his children? "When you sit in your house [formally], and when you walk by the way [informally]."

I have heard many fathers say, "I teach, but my teaching is informal. I teach when we are fishing. I teach when we are in the car or at the ball game." Bible teaching should be informal, but we shouldn't use this as an excuse to ignore formal teaching. Some fear formal, structured teaching. *If I make my children sit down to rigid, formal instruction, they will reject the faith.*

But we don't learn arithmetic the informal way. We don't learn English or chemistry the informal way. Why? It doesn't work. No, we rigorously attend class, and then we come home and study. The Bible is much more important than chemistry. Eternity hangs in the balance. At death, scientific knowledge will end, but the "word of our God will stand forever" (Isa. 40:8).

Children don't reject our faith because of too much *formal* Bible teaching. They reject it because we don't practice it. They reject it because we practice it but do not value it enough to teach it to them. Or they reject it because they never receive new birth. But too much knowledge is not the problem. A lack of knowledge usually is the problem.

Our children's minds are like spiritual gardens, notes William Gurnall (1617–79), one of the great seventeenth-century Puritan preachers. "This is the difference between religion and atheism; religion doth not grow without planting, but will die even where it is planted without watering. Atheism, irreligion, and profaneness are weeds that will grow without setting, but they will not die without plucking up."

Gurnall was right. No garden is a vacuum. Something grows. Untended ground—untaught minds—will yield weeds. But we want fruit, not weeds, and fruit grows only by planting, weeding, and fertilizing with great persistence. If you don't want weeds, you must teach your children regularly and intentionally.

Maybe you are thinking, *That is why I send them to Christian school. The school will teach my children the Bible.* Christian schools can help, but they can never replace Dad (or the parent in a single-parent home). They can wonderfully supplement a dad who is already teaching his children, but they will seldom effectively replace him. Although most parents think peers have the greatest influence on their teenage children, the social research indicates otherwise: "An extensive study of 272,400 teenagers conducted by *USA Today Weekend Magazine* found that 70% of teens identified their parents as the most important influence in their lives."[4]

A friend recently spoke to the student body at a Christian high school. He left discouraged. Despite a first-class faculty dedicated to teaching from a biblical worldview, he could discern little spiritual difference between these young adults and those at the nearby public school. Why? In most cases, the fathers had hired the school to do the job that God has commanded them to do, and God was not blessing the abdication.

Fathers, you and I are the gardeners. We cannot be replaced. We cannot hire a school or church to replace us. We can, and probably should, hire a school to *assist* us. Our children's minds are the gardens. If we want a rugged faith, nourished by a biblical worldview, we must sweat and labor in that garden. Pull up the weeds with discipline, plant the seed of God's Word, and fertilize it with example. "If you neglect to instruct them in the way of holiness," concludes John Flavel (1627–91), "will the devil neglect to instruct them in the way of wickedness? No; if you will not teach them to pray, he will teach them to curse, swear, and lie; if ground be uncultivated, weeds will spring up."[5]

Sunday schools and youth groups cannot replace fathers either. In the first chapter we noted that 88 percent of the teens in evangelical churches will walk away from Christianity. Some 70 percent of those in church youth groups (teen Sunday school) will do the same. Parental abdication is not working. God is not blessing it. In his book *Rethink*, Steve Wright supplies an avalanche of data to support this point. For example, "88% of kids raised in Christian homes do not continue to follow the Lord after they graduate from high school."[6] Wright goes on to explain why. Parents have abdicated from their role as chief educators. Sunday schools and youth groups cannot compensate for the loss.

The Bible is clear that fathers are the primary spiritual teachers of their children. Chapter 4 described God's holiness. Chapter 5 explored his grace. These are at the heart of the gospel. The fear of God, taught by this gospel, awakens us to our responsibility. Heaven and hell hang in the balance. The fear of God is also the fountain of the wisdom and knowledge that we teach: "The fear of the LORD is the beginning of wisdom" (Prov. 9:10); "The fear of the LORD is the beginning of knowledge" (Prov. 1:7). Your children need these virtues, and they are found in the mouths of parents who fear God. Ultimately, parents obtain these virtues at the cross. The cross reveals the reason to fear God. Then it shows us the incarnation of the wisdom of God: Christ, "in whom are hidden all the treasures of wisdom and knowledge" (Col. 2:3).

WHERE IS YOUR CONFIDENCE?

A second reason that we don't teach our children is that we don't have much confidence in the message—the gospel. The more confidence parents have in the message, the more persistently they will teach. Everyone leans on somebody or something. It is our boast. It is our confidence when times get tough. Some parents trust in a particular school. Others trust in the ability of a youth leader. Some parents rely on morality. They place their children in front of a wholesome Christian video and trust that Christians will emerge. For most of us, it is more basic. We rely on ourselves—our sincerity, our wisdom, the way our parents raised us, our family traditions, or our cleverness.

But gospel-centered parents trust in the gospel. It is their confidence, their hope. The gospel "is the power of God for salvation to everyone who believes" (Rom. 1:16). They know that the Word of God is living and active. It pierces (Heb. 4:12). It provokes new birth: "You have been born again, not of perishable seed but of imperishable, through the living and abiding word of God" (1 Peter 1:23). The gospel is God's dynamite.

This is important. You cannot change your child's heart. You need power outside yourself. In the second chapter we noted that new birth is a spiritual heart transplant. When it takes place, the war is over. The rest of your parenting is just mop-up. Chapter 6 explored the power of our example, chapter 7 the father's influence over his children's hearts, and chapters 8 and 9 how to use discipline to influence our children's hearts. Now we are at the crux of the matter. Ultimately, the gospel is the decisive heart changer. Many reading these words did not grow up in Christian families, and even if they did, their parents did not apply biblical principles. Yet they heard the gospel, the power of God impacted them, and they responded. It is the same with our children.

Conversion is a supernatural event. At conversion people joyfully embrace a message repugnant to human pride. Scripture tells us that the gospel is foolishness to worldly wisdom (1 Cor. 1:18). It is offensive to human dignity (Gal. 5:11). It is a stumbling stone to the self-reliant (Rom. 9:32).

The message of the cross is the cause for most persecution (Gal. 6:12). In the same way, every child enters the world at war with the gospel. Parents face a great temptation to soften the message so that their children will accept it. But there is no way to soften this message without losing its power. There is no way to make it palatable. The power is in its offense.

Because this is true, parents repetitively preach this message because their confidence is in God and the power of his Word. They know that God has promised to bless the gospel. They know that unless God supernaturally opens their children's hearts to this message, they will remain in darkness. They believe with all their hearts that God will soften their children's hearts through this gospel. In other words, parents come to their children with the same dependence on the gospel with which Paul came to Corinth.

> And I, when I came to you, brothers, did not come proclaiming to you the testimony of God with lofty speech or wisdom. For I decided to know nothing among you except Jesus Christ and him crucified. And I was with you in weakness and in fear and much trembling, and my speech and my message were not in plausible words of wisdom, but in demonstration of the Spirit and of power, that your faith might not rest in the wisdom of men but in the power of God. (1 Cor. 2:1–5)

Confidence in these truths makes parents gospel centered. They teach their children, but all their teaching funnels down to the gospel. Why? Because the gospel is the power of God, and they need that power to reach their children.

183

Parents are not in control of the process. God alone is in control of being known. The thirteen inches from our child's head to his or her heart is the longest distance in the world. That is why John Piper writes that God "is not like the multiplication table or the table of elements; He alone is knowable as the one totally in control of being known."[7]

Parents who trust in the power of the gospel teach it to their children. They relate their dinner discussion to it. They teach it through their discipline. They attend churches that preach the gospel clearly and decisively. They center their family devotions on it. In other words, they constantly teach the contents of chapters 4 and 5, the holiness and grace of God. They relate all of life to Christ's incarnation, life, death, resurrection, and ascension. They read and teach the entire Bible to their children, but they always relate its parts to its center, to the gospel.

Finally, they never presume that their children understand the gospel. We noted in chapter 1 that parents do this at their peril. A young person started attending our church. He was from a Christian home. He had attended an evangelical church every Sunday for twenty years. Yet in a membership interview, when we asked him to articulate the gospel, he said, "It is the Ten Commandments."

When I explained this to his parents, they were astounded. They had presumed that he understood the gospel. But the default condition of our flesh is "earn it." We enter the world in love with legalism. We are convinced that we can merit God's favor. We love moralism, but we resist the gospel. Parents who understand this never cease preaching the gospel to themselves and their children.

APPLY THE GOSPEL

Teaching the gospel to our children is not enough. We must also help our children apply it. In other words, our children's ethics need to flow out of the gospel. The gospel's moral teaching is far-reaching. It shows us how to live the law of love that Jesus said summed up the Law and the Prophets (Matt. 22:37–40). It teaches us to overcome bitterness, grow in love, and conquer selfishness. Initially the gospel is about our sin and God's mercy. Then it becomes an encyclopedia that answers most ethical decisions.

Whenever your children fight, apply the gospel to their behavior. The gospel is the rationale for service. You might say something like this: "Jesus poured out his life for you. When you deserved nothing but judgment and condemnation, he was tortured to death in your place. Since Jesus did this for you, you should serve your brothers and sisters."

When your teen borrows her sister's new skirt without asking and ruins it, you will need to mediate with the gospel. It is the rationale for forgiveness. "You were Jesus' enemy when he died to forgive your sin. Your sister's sin against you is trivial by comparison. If God forgave you, certainly you should forgive your sister."

When your seventh grader is unwilling to reach out to his non-Christian friends, remind him how Jesus descended from eternal realms of glory, entered our world, and came to die for us. In the same way, he needs to leave his comfort zone for non-Christians in the neighborhood.

When your child brings home a bad report card, don't make straight A's the issue. Go for your child's heart.

Remind her that Christians do all for the glory of God (1 Cor. 10:31). That includes grades. Why? Jesus died on the cross for the glory of God. You should excel at school for the same reason.

When your athlete gets demoted to second team and wants to quit, remind him that Christians pursue team success at personal expense. Why? That is what Jesus did. He sought the lowest place that he might lift us to the highest place. He died that we might live. He was voluntarily abased that we might be exalted. Your athlete needs to die for the team's success even if it means warming the bench.

The gospel—the incarnation, life, death, and resurrection of Jesus—is our tutorial. It teaches us everything we need to know about people, God, ethics, marriage, humility, submission to authority, excellence, ambition, heaven, hell, hope, true love, and much more. The applications are almost infinite. I have been a Christian for many years, and every week I find new applications for the gospel.

TEACHING SUGGESTIONS

The last reason that we shirk our teaching responsibilities is lack of confidence in our ability. Many of you are like me. You are not trained educators. You are not good at teaching. You don't know how to teach. Practically, then, how do we instruct our children? Here is the good news. We can lack all the training of a professional educator, yet still be immensely effective with our children. What this looks like practically depends on the age of your children.

You should expect to accomplish little *formal* teaching before age five. Of course, each child is different. An unusually bright child might respond to formal teaching earlier, but this situation is exceptional. During early childhood, proficient parents establish control over their child with discipline and affection. Self-control is a prerequisite to the child's ability to learn. During this time parents read biblical picture books to their children. As the child matures, the parents control less and teach more.

In other words, effective discipline makes formal teaching possible. An undisciplined child will be difficult to teach. Use the first five years to establish the child's capacity for self-control.

I watched a mother relate to her toddler in a grocery-store aisle. The child grabbed everything in sight, and when Mom tried to restrain her, she mouthed off. She was out of control. Her mother threatened and scolded, but to no avail. The child ignored her mother, which in turn just increased Mom's embarrassment and anger.

A child in this condition will be difficult to teach. But disciplined children can sit still long enough to be taught. All of this implies the transfer of our self-control to our children through loving discipline.

Preschool children relate to pictures. Bible storybooks with big, colorful pictures are helpful. Your children will want to see the same pictures over and over again. Don't give them information that is over their heads. Here are three books that you might find helpful: *The Jesus Storybook Bible*, by Sally Lloyd-Jones; *The Big Picture Story Bible*, by David Helm; and *Dangerous Journey: The Story of Pilgrim's Progress*, by Oliver Hunkin.

In later childhood, ages five through eight, you can introduce children to picture Bibles that contain more narrative. As your child matures, less spanking and more instruction is normal. Sometime before adolescence, corporal punishment should be a thing of the past.

At about age nine or ten, you can begin reading to them from an adult Bible. Each child is different. These ages are generalizations. Be creative. Make it fun. Make it worshipful. The important thing is to respect and honor God's Word by reading it to your children. "It should be obvious, but the first duty of Christian parents is to bring children in contact with the biblical data," notes Doug Wilson. "This is done through reading the Bible, reading Bible stories, listening to Bible tapes, etc. In the second place, this is done through the reading of godly and instructive books. This includes books like *The Chronicles of Narnia*, biographies of missionaries, etc."[8]

In the late grade-school years, you can engage in deeper discussions about issues on an adult level. Apply the Bible to the daily news. What does the gospel teach us about abortion, inflation, the dignity of man, racism, relationships between the sexes, and the environment? Does the Bible say anything about the role of government, economics, the stock market, or genetic engineering? What does the Bible teach about picking a mate, dating, and marriage?

As a family, read biographies of great saints or classic works of fiction. Together as a family we enjoyed books such as *Where the Red Fern Grows*, *The Yearling*, *The Bronze Bow*, and *The Pilgrim's Progress*. After reading one of these books, we always returned to our staple, the Bible.

The best time and place to gather the family for instruction is a family meal. The meal and the teaching should be habitual. The teaching doesn't need to be long. Fifteen minutes is adequate. A family meal is a consistent time when the family is together. "In our home," adds Wilson, "the best place for godly instruction has been, not surprisingly, dinner table discussion. This is a very practical application of the instruction of Deuteronomy 6. Parents can teach vocabulary and doctrine at the same time. They can take advantage of questions. They can integrate the Word of God with what is going on around them or out in the world."[9]

Be flexible. Jonathan Edwards ate separately from his children so that he could study. But afterward, the family gathered in the parlor and Edwards tenderly taught his small charges. The important principle is a daily, consistent time together as a family. For most of us, the family meal is the ideal time.

Individualism can be the enemy of family devotions. Individualism is rampant in our culture. It can make a regular family meal almost impossible, especially when your children enter their teens. You cannot have regular family devotions unless each member of the family is willing to subordinate his or her personal desires to the greater good of the family. Selfish individualism is the unwillingness to sacrifice my wants for the good of the larger social unit, in this case the family. It is important to teach your children that the family is more important than their individual pursuits. Some will have to forgo tennis lessons, ballet practice, computer games, their favorite TV show, or time with friends to be together as a family. But saying "no" to our wants for the success of a larger social unit is a crucial lesson for all Christians to learn.

The bottom line is this: You can't teach God's Word to your family unless you meet together consistently. "Perhaps the single most important ritual a family can observe is having dinner together," notes Dr. Madeline Levine. "Families who eat together five or more times a week have kids who are significantly less likely to use tobacco, alcohol, or marijuana, have higher grade-point averages, less depressive symptoms, and fewer suicide attempts than families who eat together two or fewer times a week."[10]

Because so few families regularly share a meal, formal teaching has almost disappeared. A friend visited a Christian family during the dinner hour. The teen children grazed through the kitchen, grabbing a piece of pizza and retreating to their rooms to eat and pursue personal interests. There was no family meal, no discussion, and no social interaction. Most distressing, this night was not an exception. It was this family's norm. Formal teaching from parents will be rare in this environment.

By contrast, I know of another father who built a special dinner table with a small bookshelf under the table edge to hold each child's Bible. After the dishes were cleared, the Bibles came out for reading, discussion, and prayer. Today, these children are grown. Many are missionaries, pastors, or pastor's wives. Family devotions matter. Parents who give formal teaching to their children get results. "This practice [family devotions] is certainly an aberration," notes George Barna. "Fewer than one out of every ten born-again families read the Bible together during a typical week or pray together during a typical week."[11]

You may be thinking, *You mean I have to prepare a daily lecture for my children?* No, that is not what I mean. In fact, that is probably the worst thing you could do. Instead, teach by asking questions. This forces your children to think and interact with the Bible. Children respond to this method. Have one, or several, of the children read a portion of the Bible aloud. Then ask questions. What is this passage about? Why is it important? Does anything in this passage surprise you? How does this passage relate to the gospel? What does it tell us about God? What claim does it make on your life?

Fathers, discuss what you read in your morning devotions. It takes no preparation, and is conducive to spontaneous discussion. If you missed morning devotions, discuss the Sunday sermon, or read through a book of the Bible together. The possibilities are endless. The point is this: You don't need to be a Bible scholar or a schoolteacher to teach your children. What you need is diligence, consistency, perseverance, and confidence that repeated exposure to the gospel will ultimately change your children's lives.

Don't get discouraged. Many times I would ask questions and get little or no response:

"What was the sermon about this week?

"God."

"Could you be more specific?"

Blank stares . . .

The temptation to discouragement is great. You will experience this temptation. Parents who believe that God will bless what he has commanded persevere. They give their children repeated exposure to the gospel.

SUMMARY

Your children need the Bread of Life. You are in their lives to feed it to them. Schools and churches can help, but they cannot replace you. If you are not doing the teaching, school and church might be irrelevant at best, a waste of time and money at worst.

Put your confidence in the gospel, the Word of God, the Bread of Life. It is the power of God for salvation. Demonstrate that confidence by regularly teaching it to your children. Confirm its relevance by modeling it.

In his sermon on family government, the great Scottish preacher Robert Murray M'Cheyne (1813–43) exhorted his congregation.

> If you do not worship God in your family, you are living in positive sin; you may be quite sure you do not care for the souls of your family. If you neglected to spread a meal for your children to eat, would it not be said that you did not care for their bodies? And if you do not lead your children and servants to the green pastures of God's Word, and to seek the living water, how plain is it that you do not care for their souls? *Do it regularly*, morning and evening. It is more needful than your daily food—more needful than your work.[12]

"Do it regularly," writes M'Cheyne. How difficult this is. Most of us start well, but finish poorly. But gospel-centered parents persevere despite their failures. Faith motivates them. When they fail, they pick themselves up, ask God to forgive them, get back on track, and return to the task. The fear of the Lord motivates them to persevere. They learn the fear of the Lord at the cross.

Confronted by their inconsistency, many fathers give up. They read a book like this. They get excited. They decide to teach their children. Things work well for ten days. Then they get sidetracked. A week later they recognize the diversion and start over again. After two or three starts and stops, they get discouraged and quit altogether.

The problem is often pride. The parent didn't know himself. "Apart from me you can do nothing," Jesus said (John 15:5). The problem is that this father thought he could perform consistently without God. When he did not meet his own personal expectations, he got discouraged and quit.

Begin with realistic assumptions. Expect to fall off the wagon repeatedly, but commit to climbing back on. Don't expect to teach the Bible every day without failure. In the real world, it won't happen. If you consistently taught your children four days a week, you would be doing well.

In all of this, run to the gospel. Like your children, you are a sinner. For this reason Jesus died. You need a Savior. Run to him for motivation. When you fail, run to him for forgiveness. The Lord is "merciful and gracious, slow to anger, and abounding in steadfast love and faithfulness" (Ex. 34:6).

Through your failures, show your children what it looks like to live in the shadow of the cross.

STUDY QUESTIONS

1. Read the following texts: Gen. 18:19; Deut. 4:9–10; 11:18; Ps. 78:5–6; Prov. 24:3–4; Eph. 6:4. Who is responsible to teach our children?

2. What does it mean for parents to put their confidence in the gospel? (Hint: Read Matt. 11:27; Rom. 1:16–17; 2 Cor. 4:6.) What alternatives are we tempted to trust?

3. What does it mean to teach our children gospel ethics? How would you apply gospel ethics to a five-year-old who bit his brother? To a seventeen-year-old dating an unbeliever?

4. What does it mean for parents to model what they teach? What does this look like practically? What should parents do when they fail in front of their children?

5. Which of the common excuses for not teaching was most relevant to you? Why?

11

GOSPEL LOVE

MY WIFE, JUDY, was driving across town listening to a song about the cross. As she heard the lyrics "And in my place was lifted up to die," suddenly she experienced a lifelike impression of herself being forced onto a cross by angry, hostile people. They were pushing her body down and preparing to drive the nails into her hands. Then she felt the cross being lifted up. "I felt so alone and helpless," she said. "I felt the hostility of the crowd pressing down on me." After this experience she felt the deepest gratitude that although she deserved crucifixion, it would never happen to her. She rejoiced that Jesus had died in her place, that he had borne the Father's wrath in her stead.

A few days later she had a second experience. But this time she was in the hostile crowd forcing Christ onto the cross. She was helping them lift up the cross to ensure his slow, tortured death. It became very clear that "it was Judy, her sin, her hostility toward Christ, that brought his death to pass." She was amazed afresh that Jesus would die for someone like her.

These experiences renewed Judy in the wonder of the substitutionary atonement. It moved the truth of God's love from her head to her heart. She saw and felt the Father's affection in a new way. The cross convinced her, just as it convinces all of us, that God's love was very costly.

Most assume that all parents love their children. Nothing could be further from the truth. Some make great sacrifices for their children, but are unable to be affectionate. Others love their children possessively. Their children have become idols. Others feel great affection for their children, but are unwilling to make sacrifices for them.

The love of God latent in the gospel is the cure for these abuses. First, the gospel motivates us to love God more than our children. Until we do that, we cannot effectively love our young ones. Second, it motivates us to sacrifice for our children. Finally, the gospel motivates us to lavish affection on our children.

LOVE GOD MORE THAN YOUR CHILDREN

I remember the true story of a Christian mother in China. When her son was a toddler, the state took him away. Because she was a Christian, the communist government considered her unfit to parent. But if she would agree to renounce the gospel, the state would let her keep her son. Because she loved God more than her son, she refused.

Twenty years later she was reunited with her son. By now he was a hardened atheist. He despised his mother and her Christianity. She was devastated. For this woman, loving God was costly. We know little of such a cost in the West, but this story illustrates an important principle: We must always love God more than our children. This is what Jesus meant when he said, "If anyone comes to me and does not *hate* his own father and mother and wife and *children* and brothers and sisters, yes, and even his own life, he cannot be my disciple. Whoever does not bear his own cross and come after me cannot be my disciple" (Luke 14:26–27).

Jesus does not really want us to hate our children. We know this because in other places, he commands us to love all men, especially our children. In this passage he uses the term *hate* to attack a destructive love that often characterizes family relationships, especially parents' relationships with their children. It loves the gift of God, the child, more than God. We know that we love this way whenever we are willing to compromise God's will to please our children or enhance our relationship with them. The mother from China could have compromised and kept her son. When Jesus tells us to "hate" our children, he means that "you are to love God so much more than your children that your love for them is like hatred compared to your love for God." There is a reason for this exhortation: We love our children with God's love only to the degree that we love God more.

The gospel is the key to understanding this love. Because Jesus loved the Father more than us, he went to the cross. Jesus died to please his Father, to amplify his glory. Love for us was secondary. He loved his Father more than us, and for that reason we get the true love we really need—his atoning death in our place on the cross.

In the same way, love for Christ must dictate how we love our children. In his book *Life Together*, Dietrich Bonhoeffer suggests that Christ must always stand between us and those we love most.[1] By this he meant that God's Word, not our lusts or fears, should govern how we love our children, spouses, and so on. We relate to our children in order to please God rather than our children. We fear God's disapproval, not our children's. This is why, according to George Marsden, the Puritans constantly warned parents not to love their children too much.[2] To a culture trained in child idolatry, these are foreign ideas.

All of this matters because ultimately the goal of parenting is not your child's happiness. It is not your happiness either. It is not their academic or career success. It is not your reputation. The goal is the glory of God. This idea appears at the very beginning—in the first chapter of the Bible.

> Then God said, "Let us make man in our *image*, after our *likeness*." . . . And God said to them, "Be *fruitful and multiply* and *fill the earth* and subdue it and have dominion over the fish of the sea and over the birds of the heavens and over every living thing that moves on the earth." (Gen. 1:26–28)

God created us in his image and likeness. Then he commanded Adam and Eve to "be fruitful and multiply and fill the earth." Here is what he meant: They were to fill the earth with children displaying God's image and likeness—his glory. Birthing and raising children, whose lives imitate Christ (the glory of God), is how parents fill the earth with God's glory. This means that ultimately parenting is for the glory of God.

It is not primarily about us or our children. "Why did God create the world and mankind?" asks John Hannah. "God's chief end is to be known in all his glory . . . God values Himself above all else, and because he does, he is himself the end of creation."[3]

This matters because unless you are clear on God's purpose, unless you love God more than your children, you will not be able to effectively love your children. For example, your conscience might say, "Jimmie needs a spanking," but your sense of compassion, or fear of the child's reaction, answers, "Not now!" But if spanking is the loving thing to do, then only a love for God stronger than your feelings for your child will motivate you to love your child—that is, spank him.

A nineteen-year-old son lived in his parents' basement. The boy was unmotivated and lazy. Worse, his girlfriend had just moved in. The parents wanted to move them out, but they were worried about how this would appear to their son (and possible future daughter-in-law). When we love God more than our children, these decisions become much easier. In the end, our children get real love. Ultimately it is not about our kids. It is about something greater. Unless we love God more, our love for our children will be just self-love disguised as altruism.

LOVE CHILDREN SACRIFICIALLY

As we have seen, the gospel is the measure of God's love. It defines it, clarifies it, and glorifies it. We don't learn about God's love by looking at people. We understand it by looking at the cross. "By this we know love, that he laid down his life for us, and we ought to lay down our lives for the brothers" (1 John 3:16). Christ's death defines what God's love looks like. Gospel-centered parents see that love, and try to imitate it.

Sometimes this love hurts. Sometimes it inconveniences us. At other times it is the source of stress. It interrupts our plans. It diverts our lives. It rechannels our energies in unexpected directions. This should not surprise us. The gospel is about the love of God, the same love demonstrated at the cross, a bloody, suffering love.

One mother described it this way: "Before my baby came, I had a career. My husband and I took leisurely walks. I enjoyed a quiet time each day, and I went shopping on Saturday mornings.

"After the baby, everything changed. I reluctantly quit the job I loved, but I still had no time for myself. *What happened?* I wanted to go back, but I couldn't. I began to pity myself. Then after several months, I realized that for the first time, I was face to face with the opportunity to engage in real love, the costly love displayed by Jesus. Jesus' life and death helped me make the connection between love and sacrifice. I changed my attitude and slowly adjusted to my new life with growing joy and gratitude."

Sacrificial love affects parents in many other ways. It means that Mom and Dad can't love their children and pursue separate career agendas at the same time. My dad was a civil engineer. He had a good job. But he and my mother were united in one purpose—raising their nine children. That meant sacrifice. When money was short, my dad took an early-morning paper route. My mother could have gone to work. She had a degree in education. But that was not the best way to love our large family. So my father pushed himself out of his comfort zone. He came home at 6:00 each evening, then got up at 4:30 a.m. to deliver papers before his regular job.

Sacrificial love affects women also. Dr. Martyn Lloyd-Jones was probably the most influential preacher of the twentieth century. He was a respected medical doctor who had walked away from a promising practice to pastor a rural Welsh church. His wife, Bethan, was also a doctor. They married in the 1920s, a time when few women had medical degrees. But Bethan, hearing the Word of God and seeing the implications of the gospel, followed Christ's example. To serve her husband and their children, she set aside her medical career. Gospel-centered love is costly. It is not wrong for Mom to have a career. The issue is love—love for children. What is best for their nurturance and their salvation? The Bible assumes that the husband is the primary breadwinner. Women are uniquely equipped to nurture. When couples find their careers impacting their children negatively, they respond with love, the love revealed at the cross. It always involves sacrifice.

In his book *King Me*, Steve Farrar tells the story of James Dobson's father. He was a traveling evangelist with a growing ministry. One day his wife contacted him. She was having trouble with their sixteen-year-old son, Jim. "I need you," she said simply. Mr. Dobson sensed his duty. He probably remembered Paul's words in 2 Corinthians 4:12: "So death is at work in us, but life in you." He would need to die if his son were to live. Jesus died that we might live, and the current of that mighty river flows through the heart of every gospel-centered parent.

Mr. Dobson picked up the phone and canceled every speaking engagement on his calendar. He took a small pastorate in a neighboring state. "For the next two years, until his son graduated from high school and went off to college," explained Farrar, "he pastored the small church and mentored his growing son."[4] When James went off to college, Mr. Dobson tried to return to his career, but the momentum had been lost. "His decision cost him dearly in terms of his career and calling. . . . The decision to go home had come at a great price."[5] Mr. Dobson died to his ambitions. But his death meant life for his son, and through his son life for the twentieth-century church. Wherever you find spiritual life, someone has usually died.

God's love will forfeit a promotion that might mean a disadvantageous move. If necessary, it will put golf on the shelf until the children are raised. A one-career family might mean camping instead of the deluxe cabin at the lake. The world tells parents to demand their rights, pursue their careers, and sacrifice others (spouse and children) to pursue selfish ambitions. But the gospel says, "You have no rights, only responsibilities." It says, "Life proceeds out of death." It says, "Your children will live to the degree of your dying."

Here is the good news: Gospel love doesn't bring life just to the child. It also imparts God's life to the parent who dies. The promises are lavish. "For the joy that was set before him [Jesus] endured the cross" (Heb. 12:2). "Whoever loses his life for my sake will find it" (Matt. 16:25). Out of death comes life to both parent and child. Do you really believe this? Gospel-centered parents do.

This is how children internalize God's love. They watch their parents modeling it. It is how they internalize their duty to love others. They absorb God's life through their parents' self-denying love.

Everything I have said in this book presupposes a willingness to love our children sacrificially. If our marriages are going to preach the gospel to our children (chapter 6), it means that Dad must become a servant-leader and that Mom must encourage and submit to his leadership. For both, this means death to the self-life.

Disciplining children (chapters 8 and 9) requires sacrificial love. It mandates consistency. Mom will have to put dinner preparation aside to discipline an unruly child, or Dad will have to turn off his favorite football game. But gospel-centered parents serve their children with one eye on the cross.

Providing spiritual food for our children (chapter 10) is costly. It means that the whole family will have to sacrifice their agendas to have a regular meal together. Mom and Dad must sacrifice to open their Bibles and teach their children when they would rather do something else.

Sacrificial love is also incarnational. It motivates parents to enter their children's world. Jesus left realms of infinite glory to save us. He entered our fallen world. Gospel-centered parents do the same. When my eldest son was in junior high, he became interested in tennis. So I took up tennis. I entered his world. My youngest son was interested in fly-fishing, so when he entered his teens we bought float tubes and fished together. They were wonderful times. Did they involve sacrifice? Sometimes. But most of the time it was joy. In the end, I was the net beneficiary.

Where is God speaking to you? What sacrifice do you need to make for the welfare of your children?

LOVE CHILDREN AFFECTIONATELY

Affection is another important dimension of God's love. Chapters 4 and 5 suggested that God the Father is the model Parent. He is affectionate. If that is true, we should also shower our children with affection. Ultimately, we learn, feel, and comprehend the Father's affection by meditating on the cross.

As we just saw, God's love is sacrificial. It is our happiness at God's expense. God's love is bigger than affection. It begins with action but terminates in the warmth of affection. As we saw in chapter 5, the expense was *infinite*. If the measure of love is its cost, then God's love is infinite. So Paul calls it "love . . . that surpasses knowledge" (Eph. 3:19).

So God's love does not start with affection. You don't feel affection for enemies, those under your wrath. As we saw in chapters 4 and 5, that is what we were—enemies of God (Rom. 5:10).

But affection is so important to God that he sent his Son to remove the offense that separated us. He did this so that he could lavish affection on us. He wanted friendship. He wanted an affectionate relationship, but sin stood in the way, so he dealt with the sin issue at the cross. He did this to open the floodgates of affection.

This is important because sometimes it is hard to feel affection for our children. Some are easy to like. Others are more difficult. Both are God's gift to us. One child is grateful, kindhearted, and compliant. Another is ungrateful, ambitious, and inattentive. One gets good grades. Another couldn't care less. One shares your interests. Another does not. One marries the person you like. Another rejects your counsel.

God sends us difficult children to test our capacity to love like our heavenly Father—to be affectionate with the disagreeable. No one knows whether you love the disagreeable child. Your affection, or its lack, takes place behind closed doors. You can fail to be affectionate with a difficult child and no one will know (except God). Or you can be affectionate with that child because you see how God has been affectionate with you—despite your unworthiness.

Parental affection is very powerful. It makes the parent, and the parent's God, attractive. It communicates love and acceptance. We might tell our children that we love them, but affection convinces them. It is the bridge over which love passes to our children. Affection is the hammer that drives the nail of truth deep into their hearts. It would be hard to overstate the importance of affection.

In his best-selling book *How to Really Love Your Child*, Dr. Ross Campbell writes, "Discipline is immeasurably easier when the child feels genuinely loved. . . . If a child does not feel genuinely loved and accepted . . . he has real difficulty identifying with his parents and their *values*."[6] As we saw in chapter 2, the point of discipline is to implant our values and beliefs in our child's heart. Campbell's point is this: Unless children feel their parents' love and acceptance, they will probably not internalize the lessons you are trying to teach them. Your worldview will not penetrate their hearts. The baton will not be transferred. Affection communicates love to your children— a love that is biblical.

The cross stirred Paul's affections. So he exhorted the Roman church to "love one another with brotherly affection" (Rom. 12:10). He yearned for the Philippians with the "affection of

Christ" (Phil. 1:8). He assumed that the effect of the gospel on the churches he planted was mutual affection for one another (Phil. 2:1). Let's pause to discuss more deeply why affection matters and then discuss some practical ways to show affection.

Affection is especially powerful when it comes from fathers. A mountain of social research highlights the crucial role of Dad's affection. It impacts a child's heart in a way that Mom's just does not. It has great power to shape and sanctify children.

The evangelist James Robison, in his weighty little book *In Search of a Father*, using the term *nurturance* instead of *affection*, writes: "Nurturance is one of the key ingredients in the socialization of the child. Without it, a child may *seem* to assimilate the values taught by the parents [father] without actually adopting them. Proper nurturance prepares the child mentally and emotionally to accept moral tenets and correct patterns for relationships with other people."[7] In other words, the more affectionate a father, the more likely that his children will internalize his values. By contrast, children tend to reject the values of unaffectionate fathers.

The father's affection, or lack thereof, influences children in other ways. Did you know that fathers (not mothers) are primarily responsible for the formation of compassion in their children? In his book *Life without Father*, social researcher David Popenoe writes: "Fathers who spent time with their children more than twice a week, giving meals, baths, and other basic care, reared the most compassionate adults. This single factor accounted for a greater percentage of the adult outcome (of empathy) than the three strongest maternal predictors combined."[8] In other words, the presence of a nurturing, affectionate father affects the internalization of compassion in children more than their mother's affection. This is important because we assume the opposite—that Mom's affection determines a child's capacity to show affection.

The father's affection, or its lack, also uniquely impacts his children's long-term happiness. Popenoe adds, "Young adults who feel emotionally close to their fathers tend to be happier and more satisfied in life, regardless of their feelings toward their mothers."[9] Henry Biller, the noted sociologist, observed that "boys who were able to confide in their fathers were likely to have high self-esteem. . . , The early father-child relationship is particularly important for the child's self-esteem. Among adolescents, those who were father absent had lower self-esteem than those who were father present, especially when father absence had begun in early childhood."[10]

The father's affection, or lack, also has a strong and lasting bearing on the child's sexual identity. According to research cited by Robison, both boys and girls form their sexual identities by relating to their father. And the more affectionate the father, the stronger the normal sex typing. The less affectionate and distant a father, the more likely his children are to be tempted with homosexuality or sexual promiscuity.[11] In *Growing Up Straight*, Peter and Barbara Wyden's insightful study on the causes of homosexuality, the authors conclude, "I never saw a homosexual who had a good relationship with his father. We have come to the conclusion that a constructive, supportive, warmly related father *precludes* the possibility of a homosexual son. It is the loving *quality* of the fathering which a boy receives, and sometimes even the mere memory of it as reinforced by the mother (when the father is deceased), that now turns out to be a vital factor. Sons must be able to admire and identify with their fathers in order to become well-adjusted heterosexual males."[12] Obviously, there are many exceptions to this data, but they are just that, exceptions.

Other studies confirm the same principle for daughters. "Inappropriate and/or inadequate fathering is a major factor in the development of homosexuality in females as well as in males. Bene (1965) reported that female homosexuals felt their fathers were weak and incompetent. The homosexual women were more hostile toward and afraid of their fathers than the heterosexual women were."[13]

Appropriate affection has a final effect. We have already mentioned it, but it is so important that it bears repeating. It makes parental discipline work! It is hard to overdiscipline children if you balance discipline with affection. Tedd Tripp calls the parent who wields his or her authority in an atmosphere of lavish affection the "benevolent despot" (probably not a good name). He describes how many children between the age of 10 and 12 have already left home mentally. "Parents who are 'benevolent despots' do not usually find their children racing to leave home. Children rarely run from a home where their needs are met. Who would want to walk out on a relationship in which he feels loved and respected?"[14] Affection is an important way to make our children feel "loved and respected."

WAYS TO SHOW AFFECTION

What are the best ways to show affection to our children? Dr. Ross Campbell suggests focused attention, eye contact, and physical touch.[15] I want to add a fourth principle: the importance of identifying evidences of grace in our children.

For many men, affection is not natural. The hard, competitive realities of life have frozen their emotions. Other fathers express affection awkwardly. The ease with which our wives show affection mystifies us. Some feel inadequate by comparison. Some men feel this way because they themselves have not been around affectionate men.

The first way to show affection is with focused attention. Focused attention is time alone with a child. When a parent gives focused attention, he or she eliminates competing distractions. For example, taking your teenage son to a men's breakfast at church is not focused attention. A family activity with other children present is not focused attention. The child might get our attention, but it won't be focused. Focused attention is exclusive time with that child. It communicates genuine love. Backpacking alone with him in the Idaho wilderness is focused attention. A special meal with your daughter at a local restaurant is focused attention.

When my children were small, I made times of focused attention a priority. We called them "special times." Each week a different child's turn came up. I would schedule an exclusive time with that child. I put it on my calendar so that I wouldn't forget. I let the child choose the place. Sometimes we went to Baskin-Robbins for ice cream. Sometimes we just took a walk to the local grocery store to buy the child's favorite candy bar.

During these times we talked about important issues. Often the children themselves brought them up. Once my eldest daughter, Sarah, and I were walking to the grocery store when she was about seven, and we passed the decomposing body of a robin on the sidewalk. Out of curiosity, she stopped to examine it. Using this opportunity, I turned the conversation to death, explaining that, like the robin, we would also someday die and decompose. Then I explained that God would one day raise our bodies and make them like Christ's body. Sarah, now an adult, still remembers that conversation.

As my children matured, I dreamed up more sophisticated special times. I took them to breakfast at the local pancake house, to their favorite fast-food restaurant, or with me on an out-of-town business trip. Focused attention is critical. It communicates affection, and unless we schedule it into our busy lives, it won't happen. Focused attention implies listening. This can be difficult for a busy father. It was often a struggle for me. Sometimes it took all my willpower. Even then I often listened poorly. But God compensated for my inadequacies. It takes time and energy to give focused attention, but the effort will be returned a hundredfold.

The second way to communicate affection is with eye contact. This means that you look your child in the eye, and listen. It means that you give him or her undivided attention. I have often failed here as well, but I have tried, and again God has compensated for my failings.

Children will ask for your attention at awkward times. You walk in from work keyed up. You just want to relax. You collapse onto the sofa, open the paper, and are interrupted by your teenage daughter, who wants to talk about a peer who doesn't like her. This is not what you wanted. What does the cross demand? Put down the paper, make eye contact, and listen. If you are like me, you make an appointment after dinner, when you can make eye contact and listen carefully.

Parents, I testify that you can fall off the wagon and climb back on because I have repeatedly failed and climbed back on. After each failure I have asked my children's forgiveness and tried again.

A third way to show affection is with appropriate physical contact. That means hugging, appropriate touching, or holding. In this age of child abuse, physical affection is often misunderstood or even avoided. A child should feel completely secure in the arms of his or her father or mother. Tragically, this is not always the case.

Effective parents, especially fathers, take every opportunity to communicate physical affection and never stop. Fathers and mothers should go out of their way to look for opportunities to express it. When my children were little, I would hold them as I read stories to them. Most of the social research shows that small children would rather be held by their fathers than their mothers.[16] There is something compelling about the size and muscularity of a man that makes children feel secure.

Boys need physical affection as much as girls. My one-year-old grandson already knows how to bring his favorite book to his mom or dad so that he can sit in his parent's lap and hear a story. Wrestle on the floor with your toddlers. Carry them in your arms. When you watch TV, put them in your lap instead of on the sofa. Carry them on your shoulders at the park. After the game, hug your Little Leaguer to celebrate the joy of victory or to show compassion in the agony of defeat. Use every opportunity to express physical affection.

There is an old superstition that this kind of father-son affection causes homosexuality. In fact, as we have seen, it is usually the *absence* of this warm man-to-man (or mom-to-man) contact that hastens homosexuality. When your son or daughter enters his or her teens, don't stop. Many parents minimize physical contact with their adolescents. When Dad's little girl hits puberty, he backs off. But this is a big mistake. Is there any period of greater insecurity than the teen years? Just when the young adult most needs her parents' physical reassurance, many quit giving it. Look for every opportunity to give hugs, pats on the back, or an arm over the shoulder. When your high school student is laboring over his homework, put your hand on his shoulder and tell him you love him. The touch makes the difference.

A fourth way to demonstrate affection is with verbal encouragement. C. J. Mahaney of Sovereign Grace Ministries calls it pointing out evidences of grace. Although there are times when you must criticize, the emphasis should be on encouragement.

Most parents find it easy to see their children's faults, but hard to see their virtues. Why is this? If you ask a parent to list a child's faults, the list will come quickly. But if you ask the parent to identify evidences of God's grace in that child, the list will often come slowly after hard thought, if at all. Why?

One reason is that we think much about our children's faults and little about their virtues. This is especially true for difficult children. But the difficult child is usually the one who most needs our affirmation. A friend asked a mother for the first thing she thought of when a particular child came to mind. She told me later that only negative words came to mind, and it disturbed her.

A second reason it is difficult to evidence grace is that we take God's grace for granted. We have not learned to be thankful for our children, despite their problems. We think we deserve better. We are ungrateful. A lack of gratitude always points to pride. It says, "I deserve good from God's hand." The gospel speaks a different message. We deserve crucifixion. We don't deserve obedient, easy children.

Words of affirmation are powerful. The Bible stresses the awesome power of the tongue. "The mouth of the righteous *is a fountain of life*" (Prov. 10:11). Appropriate words encourage, impart love, inspire, and charge our children with confidence to face tomorrow. This is especially true when we verbally identify where God is working in their lives.

Behind almost every child's weakness is a corresponding strength. After you have disciplined the weakness, take a moment to identify the strength. The child who is fearful and sensitive might also be good at making friends. The child who is defiant and strong willed is probably good at resisting peer pressure. The child who talks too much might have potential to be a good teacher. Learn to verbally and repeatedly identify God's grace in your children's lives.

What are we more aware of, their failings or God's grace? Parents deeply aware of their own sin are very sensitive to God's grace in others. Despite their children's shortcomings, they are grateful, and they express that gratitude repeatedly. But proud, self-righteous parents are slow to see God's grace at work in their children. They are demanding. They are not grateful. Nothing done by their children is good enough.

SUMMARY

Love matters. Every suggestion for parenting mentioned in this book must be bathed in love. The gospel defines that love, and the gospel motivates that love.

Before we can love our children, we must love God more. That is because love for God defines *how* we love our children. Once we settle this issue, we are equipped to love our children sacrificially. The cross calls this love out.

In addition, gospel-centered love terminates in affection. God paid a great price to be affectionate. Affection matters greatly, especially from fathers. If we want to transfer our baton to the next generation, if we want our children to adopt our faith and values, form a healthy sexual identity, obtain the confidence to achieve, and learn compassion, parents must practice the art of affection.

Paying focused attention, practicing eye contact, giving physical affection, and learning to identify evidences of grace in our children are four ways to express the affection that changes lives.

STUDY QUESTIONS

1. What was this chapter all about? Sum it up in your own words.

2. Can you think of a time when you have been tempted to compromise God's will to please your children? When parents do this, is it possible that they are really hating their children when they think they are loving them? Why or why not?

3. What would be a symptom that you are not loving your children sacrificially? In your particular situation, what would sacrificial love look like?

4. This chapter mentioned four ways to show affection. Which do you need to work on the most? How do you plan to do so?

5. According to this chapter, what practical benefits does the appropriate expression of parental affection bring children?

6. In your opinion, why is it so hard for parents to point out evidences of grace in their children's lives? Which expressions of affection are easiest for you? Which are most difficult?

12

AMAZING GRACE

ANITA CAME TO ME, overwhelmed with guilt and despair. Her daughter had driven her to the brink, and she was almost ready to fall off. Her daughter was unusually strong willed, and Anita didn't know how to control her. She found herself increasingly angry. She knew she shouldn't be, but she didn't know how to change. She felt defeated.

I gave her some practical advice, and then finished with, "Rest in the grace of God."

Parents need grace. There are many things to do, and most of us are not doing them consistently. In Jerry Bridges's words, we need to preach the gospel to ourselves daily.[1] Despite numerous failures, parents who do this will walk in increasing freedom from condemnation and discouragement. They will also model how to walk in gospel victory for their children, and children need to see their parents doing just that.

FAILURE

We are sinners. We fail. This book has presented us with a list of "shoulds" and "should nots." None of us do them all consistently. Then when we do, we overdo it.

Bill could not control his very strong-willed thirteen-year-old son. He came to me with tremendous guilt. Several times Bill had lost his temper, had yelled abusively, and had even disciplined too harshly. He knew the importance of his example and felt devastated by his failure to be patient and affectionate. I pointed him to the gospel. It was Bill's solution, his refuge. Jesus had died to atone for his anger. He was clothed in Christ's righteousness. Jesus had freed him from the need to be perfect. I exhorted Bill to ask his son's forgiveness, which he had already done, and walk in the glorious freedom provided by the gospel.

Yes, God is holy. Our sin is serious. The cross is the measure of sin's horrors. Yet here is the miracle: God loves us. Jesus bore God's wrath in our place.

When my eldest daughter turned fourteen, she went through an obnoxious stage. She was difficult to be around. She needed her dad to be patient, kind, and accessible. But I failed the test. One day I lost it. I grabbed the spanking stick (still being used on her eight-year-old brother), bent her over the kitchen counter, and spanked her. My action was inappropriate. She was past the spanking stage. I had reacted in sinful anger. I felt tremendous guilt. I needed grace, and the gospel was the solution. Again, I preached the gospel to myself, I asked Sarah to forgive me, and we moved on with life. (We have a delightful friendship today.)

Here is the important point: When we turn to the gospel, it transforms our weaknesses. "My grace is sufficient for you," Jesus told Paul, "for my power is made perfect in weakness" (2 Cor. 12:9). God has inserted his treasure (the gospel of the glory of God in the face of Christ), the light that converts our children, "in jars of clay." We are those clay pots! He has done this "to show that the surpassing power belongs to God and not to us" (2 Cor. 4:7). What wonderful news! God uses the imperfect efforts of gospel-centered parents to do his deep and abiding work in our children. In the meantime, the gospel frees us from the burden of perfection.

Parents who repeatedly find forgiveness in the gospel can extend that forgiveness to their children. Your children need to watch you continually shedding your guilt and fear at the foot of the cross.

CONCLUSION

This book has given us much to do. We must teach our children. Delegating that task to others will not work unless we are first doing it at home.

Fathers are the chief parents. Their wives are their assistants. Dads, we need to get off the couch and actively engage our children.

Our marriages preach to our children. Husbands should be servant-leaders. Wives should joyfully submit to their leadership.

We should discipline our children's heart-sins, and discipline them consistently. We should patiently use discipline to teach the gospel. We should regularly gather our families and teach our children the gospel.

Here is the problem: You and I do not measure up. Does this mean that we should give up and not try? No, the gospel frees us to fail and continually reapply ourselves to an impossible standard. Why? God knows we cannot be perfect. His Son paid the price for our imperfections. He lived the perfect life in our place. Faith credits his perfections to us.

So the gospel not only teaches us how to parent. The gospel salves the wounds of our imperfections, and it encourages us to persevere through our failures.

> Amazing grace!—how sweet the sound—
>   that saved a wretch like me!
> I once was lost, but now am found,
>   was blind, but now I see.[2]

The gospel is about grace. It is about grace that is truly amazing. For weak and needy parents, it is good news indeed. Apply it to your conscience daily! Your children will be the beneficiaries.

NOTES

Introduction

1. George Barna, *Revolutionary Parenting* (Carol Stream, IL: Tyndale, 2007), xi.

Chapter One: Intellectual Submarines

1. Francis Schaeffer, *How Should We Then Live?* (Westchester, IL: Crossway, 1976), 19.

2. Tim Kimmel, *Grace-Based Parenting* (Nashville: Thomas Nelson, 2004), 12–13.

3. Christian Smith and Melinda Lundquist Denton, *Soul Searching* (New York: Oxford University Press, 2005).

4. Gene Edward Veith, "A Nation of Deists," *WORLD*, June 25, 2005. "After interviewing over 3,000 teenagers, the social scientists summed up their beliefs: (1) 'A god exists who created and ordered the world and watches over human life on earth.' (2) 'God wants people to be good, nice, and fair to each other, as taught in the Bible and by most world religions.' (3) 'The central goal of life is to be happy and to feel good about oneself.' (4) 'God does not need to be particularly involved in one's life except when God is needed to resolve a problem.' (5) 'Good people go to heaven when they die.'"

5. Ibid.

6. Mark Regnerus *Forbidden Fruit* (New York: Oxford University Press, 2007).

7. Gene Edward Veith, "Sex and the Evangelical Teen," *WORLD*, August 11, 2007, 9.

8. Regnerus, *Forbidden Fruit,* 154.

9. Tom Bisset, *Why Christian Kids Leave the Faith* (Grand Rapids: Discovery House Publishers, 1992), quoted in Timothy Sisemore, *World-Proof Your Kids* (Fearn, UK: Christian Focus, 2007), 26.

10. A. W. Pink, *The Sovereignty of God* (1928; repr., Edinburgh: Banner of Truth, 1993), 79.

11. Stephen Smallman, *Spiritual Birthline* (Wheaton, IL: Crossway, 2006), 142.

Chapter Two: Gospel-Powered Parenting

1. "Parenting," *Wikipedia, The Free Encyclopedia,* http://en.wikipedia. org/w/index.php?title=Parenting&oldid=300836102.

2. This is why God's Word places so many fences around sexual morality. When a man and woman conceive a child, a conscious life begins that will never end. To increase the influence on the side of salvation, God wants each infant to have both a father and a mother, committed to each other for life, raising the child in the fear of God. Influence and encouragement from both parents increases the likelihood that salvation is taking place.

3. Tedd Tripp, *Shepherding a Child's Heart* (Wapwallopen, PA: Shepherd Press, 1995), 5.

4. See his helpful exposé of sin, *Not the Way It's Supposed to Be* (Grand Rapids: Eerdmans, 1995).

5. R. C. Sproul, *Saved from What?* (Wheaton, IL: Crossway, 2002).

Chapter Three: Gospel Fear

1. Edward T. Welch, *When People Are Big and God Is Small* (Phillipsburg, NJ: P&R Publishing, 1997), 96.

2. Ibid., 98. Welch's book is an excellent primer on the fear of God. I have found no better definition of the fear of God than the one in chapter 6 of this book.

Chapter Four: A Holy Father

1. Os Guinness, *Fit Bodies, Fat Minds* (Grand Rapids: Baker, 1994), 10.

2. Rodney Stark, *The Victory of Reason* (New York: Random House, 2005).

3. Philip Ryken, *Exodus* (Wheaton, IL: Crossway, 2005), 82, emphasis mine.

4. D.A. Carson et al, eds., *The New Bible Commentary* (Downers Grove, IL: InterVarsity Press, 1994). See the notes on Leviticus 11:1.

5. A. W. Tozer, *The Knowledge of the Holy* (New York: Harper and Row, 1961), 110.

6. Ibid., 111.

7. Wayne Grudem, *Systematic Theology* (Grand Rapids: Zondervan, 1994), 568.

8. Bart Campolo, "The Limits of God's Grace," *Journal of Student Ministries* (Sept/Oct 2006). Also see http://pastorbrouwer.wordpress.com/2006/11/18/bad-theology-by-bart-campolo/.

9. Jerry Bridges, *The Gospel for Real Life* (Colorado Springs: NavPress, 2003), 52.

10. Leon Morris, *The Atonement* (Downers Grove, IL: InterVarsity Press, 1983), 153, 155.

11. A. W. Pink, *The Attributes of God* (Grand Rapids: Baker, 1975), 77.

12. Martyn Lloyd-Jones, *The Cross* (Wheaton, IL: Crossway, 1986), 76.

13. Jonathan Edwards, "The Wisdom of God Displayed in Salvation," in *The Works of Jonathan Edwards* (Edinburgh: Banner of Truth, 1995), 2:145.

14. Timothy Lane and Paul David Tripp, *How People Change* (Greensboro, NC: New Growth Press, 2006), 5.

Chapter Five: A Gracious Father

1. John Frame, *The Doctrine of God* (Phillipsburg, NJ: P&R Publishing, 2002), 426.

2. William Hendriksen, *Commentary on I and II Timothy and Titus* (Edinburgh: Banner of Truth, 1957), 370.

3. Martyn Lloyd-Jones, *The Cross* (Wheaton, IL: Crossway, 1986), 75.

4. J. I. Packer, *Knowing God* (Downers Grove, IL: InterVarsity Press, 1973), 132. For anyone skeptical about the contents of this chapter, chapter 13 in *Knowing God* is about the grace of God and is a wonderful read.

5. John Piper, *Desiring God* (Sisters, OR: Multnomah, 2003). For more on God's happiness in himself, read the first chapter of *Desiring God*.

6. John Piper, *The Pleasures of God* (Portland: Multnomah, 1991), 48–49.

7. John Piper, *God's Passion for His Glory* (Wheaton, IL: Crossway, 1998). This book is an immense resource for more on this important question and its answer. It contains the entire text of Jonathan Edwards's seminal work *A Dissertation on the End for Which God Created the World*. It also includes four very helpful introductory chapters by Piper. Edwards's work completely reoriented my Christian thought and experience.

8. The texts confirming this conclusion are voluminous, and most of them are from the mouth of Jesus himself. He talked of hell as chaff burning with unquenchable fire (Mal. 4:1; Matt. 3:12; Luke 16:23–24; John 15:6). The New Testament describes hell as a fiery furnace where its citizens constantly weep and gnash their teeth (Ps. 21:8–9; Matt. 13:42, 50; 22:13–14; Mark 9:43–49; Luke 16:23–24; Rev. 14:10; 19:20; 20:10–15; 21:8ff.). Jesus described hell as eternal

fire prepared for the Devil and his angels (Matt. 25:41) and a place of conscious torment (Mark 9:48; Luke 16:23–24). Paul described it as everlasting destruction, shut out from the presence of God (2 Thess. 1:9), and Jesus described it as eternal punishment (Matt. 25:45–46).

9. Jerry Bridges and Bob Bevington, *The Great Exchange* (Wheaton, IL: Crossway, 2007), 118.

10. Iain Murray, *The Old Evangelicalism* (Edinburgh: Banner of Truth, 2005), 76.

11. Jerry Bridges, *The Joy of Fearing God* (Colorado Springs: Waterbrook, 1997), is an excellent study for those wishing to further explore the fear of God. Another valued recommendation is Ed Welch's wonderful study *When People Are Big and God Is Small* (Phillipsburg, NJ: P&R Publishing, 1997). Chapter 6 defines the fear of God. It is the best definition that I have yet seen.

Chapter Six: The First Principle of Parenting

1. This is why "doing," not teaching, is the first requirement for an elder or deacon (1 Tim. 3:2–5). Paul's concern is his example, not his oratorical gifts. Example is also the first priority for a pastor. "Keep a close watch on *yourself* and on the teaching" (1 Tim. 4:16). Again, notice the order. First Paul told Timothy to watch himself, *then* to watch his teaching. In the same way, Paul warned the elders at Ephesus, "Pay careful attention to *yourselves* and to all the flock, in which the Holy Spirit has made you overseers" (Acts 20:28). Again, the order is instructive. First, pay attention to yourself—your holiness, godliness, love, humility, and so on—then pay attention to the holiness and godliness of the church. Therefore, Peter tells his elders to "shepherd the flock of God . . . being examples to the flock" (1 Peter 5:2–3).

2. Alexander Strauch, *Biblical Eldership* (Littleton, CO: Lewis and Roth, 1995), 70.

3. Dave Harvey, *Am I Called?*, Sovereign Grace Perspectives Series (Gaithersburg, MD: Sovereign Grace Ministries, 2005), 26–27.

4. J. C. Ryle, *The Duties of Parents* (1888; repr., Sand Springs, OK: Grace and Truth Books, 2002), 27–28.

5. Weldon Hardenbrook, *Missing in Action* (Ben Lomond, CA: Conciliar Press, 1996), 176.

6. G. A. Pritchard, *Willow Creek Seeker Services* (Grand Rapids: Baker, 1996), 290.

7. Paul David Tripp, *Age of Opportunity* (Phillipsburg, NJ: P&R Publishing, 2001), 67, emphasis mine.

Chapter Seven: Gospel Fathers

1. *Albert Mohler Program,* July 14, 2008.

2. George Gilder, *Men and Marriage* (Gretna, LA: Pelican, 1986), initially published as *Sexual Suicide* (New York: Quadrangle, 1973). In the 1970s Gilder argued persuasively that if wives/mothers assumed the roles of provider, leader, and parent, men would respond by increasingly abandoning home and family. Unfortunately, he was a prophet, for that is exactly what has happened for the last thirty years.

3. Ibid.

4. The literature to support this statement is massive. For example, a recent study in Phillip Longman, "Why Men Rule—And Conservatives Will Inherit the Earth," *Foreign Policy* (March-April 2006), notes that population decline in the West can be traced directly to the collapse of fatherhood in Western culture. When a culture does not honor fatherhood, men abandon ship, fail to marry, and fail to procreate. Longman goes on to point out that the segments of society that do not honor fatherhood are not reproducing.

5. Nancy Gibbs, "Father," *Time,* June 28, 1993, 53.

6. Ibid.

7. Robbie Low, "The Truth about Men & Church," *Touchstone*, June 2003, http://touchstonemag.com/archives/print.php?id=16-05-024-v.

8. Ibid.

9. See Ps. 10:14; 68:5; 146:9; Jer. 49:11. One of the great sins against social justice was oppression of the fatherless (Isa. 1:17, 23; 10:2; Jer. 5:28; 22:3; Zech. 7:10). God promises to judge it (Mal. 3:5).

10. Statement of Dr. Urie Bronfenbrenner from Cornell University cited in Dr. Wade Horn, "Lunacy 101: Questioning the Need for Fathers," quoting Dr. Urie Bronfenbrenner, *The Jewish World Review*, July 7, 1999, http://www.jewishworldreview.com/cols/horn.html.

11. Stuart Birks, "Effects of Fatherlessness (US data)," *Fatherhood Initiative*, January 24, 1996, http://www.massey.ac.nz/~kbirks/gender/econ/nodad.htm.

12. David Popenoe, *Life without Father* (New York: The Free Press, 1996), 151–52, cites studies showing that children who lack a father due to death turn out little different than children who grow up in the same home with their biological father. The statistics are radically different, however, when children are deprived of their father through divorce or the failure of their mother to marry the father.

13. Chuck Colson, "Rebuilding the Foundations of Fatherhood," http://www.crosswalk.com/1350449/.

14. Edwards's biographer notes, "At the core of Edwards' outlook is a rigorously unsentimental view of love. This attitude is especially difficult to appreciate for those whose sensibilities have been shaped by the sentimentality of the decades that have succeeded." See George Marsden, *Jonathan Edwards: A Life* (New Haven: Yale University Press, 2003), 137.

15. Ann Douglas, *The Feminization of American Culture* (1977; repr., London: Papermac, 1996). See especially chapter 4, "The Loss of Theology: From Dogma to Fiction."

16. H. Richard Niebuhr, *The Kingdom of God in America* (Chicago: Willet, Clark & Company, 1937), 193. Quoted in ibid., 18.

17. Stephen J. Nichols, *Jesus Made in America* (Downers Grove, IL: InterVarsity Press, 2008).

18. Ann Douglas, "The Loss of Theology," in *The Feminization of American Culture* (1977; repr., London: Papermac, 1996).

19. John Tierney, "As Barriers Disappear, Some Gender Gaps Widen," *New York Times*, September 8, 2008, http://www.nytimes.com/2008/09/09/science/09tier.html?scp=1&sq=johntierneymars venusstereotypes&st=cse.

20. Steve Maynard, "In God They Trust, Despite It All," *Tacoma News Tribune*, March 23, 2008.

21. David Murrow, *Why Men Hate Going to Church* (Nashville: Thomas Nelson, 2005), 8, 41, 43, 59.

22. This statement is reputed to have come from C. S. Lewis.

23. James Dobson, "Two Mommies Is One Too Many," *Time*, December 12, 2006, http://www.time.com/time/magazine/article/0,9171,1568485,00.html

24. See James Robison, *In Search of a Father* (Carol Stream, IL: Tyndale, 1979), 159. Also see Peter Wyden and Barbara Wyden, *Growing Up Straight* (Lanham, MD: Stein and Day, 1968), 60–61; Ross Campbell, *How to Really Love Your Child* (Wheaton, IL: Victor, 1985), 80–81.

25. David Wegener, review of *Fatherless America*, by David Blakenhorn, *Journal for Biblical Manhood and Womanhood* 3 (Fall 1998):13.

26. Alan Barron, "Fatherless Families," *Manhood*, http://manhood.com.au/manhood.nsf/f5d5a3b4a7ee9a474a256a770046651d/a4f 30298b6a6fd72ca256e77002ea78f!OpenDocument (accessed May 22, 2008).

27. Stuart Scott, *Think Biblically*, ed. John MacArthur (Wheaton, IL: Crossway, 2003), 161. This is an excellent discussion of both biblical masculinity and biblical femininity.

28. Gilder, *Men and Marriage*.

Chapter Eight: Foundations of Discipline, Sin, and Authority

1. Timothy Sisemore, *World-Proof Your Kids* (Fearn, UK: Christian Focus, 2007), 6.

2. R.C. Sproul, "The Pelagian Captivity of the Church," *Modern Reformation* 10, no. 3 (May/June 2001): 22–29.

3. Paul David Tripp, *Age of Opportunity* (Phillipsburg, NJ: P&R Publishing, 1997), 45.

4. Leslie Margolin, "Child Abuse by Mothers' Boyfriends: Why the Overrepresentation?" *Child Abuse and Neglect* 16 (1992): 541–51. In a British study, the incidence of child abuse was twenty times higher for children living with their cohabiting parents and thirty-three times higher among children living with their mother and her boyfriend compared to children living with their biological, married parents. See *Broken Homes and Battered Children: A Study of the Relationship between Child Abuse and Family Type* (London: Family Education Trust, 1993).

5. Steve Farrar, *King Me* (Chicago: Moody, 2005), 36.

6. George Barna, *Revolutionary Parenting* (Carol Stream, IL: Tyndale, 2007), 83.

7. Bruce Ware, *Father, Son, and Holy Spirit* (Wheaton, IL: Crossway, 2005), 137.

8. The New Testament texts exhorting us about submission to authority are numerous and lengthy. Why? Because this subject matters greatly to God (Rom. 13:1-7; Eph. 5:22–6:9; Col. 3:18-4:1; 1 Peter 2:13–3:7).

Chapter Nine: Discipline That Preaches

1. Paul David Tripp, *Instruments in the Redeemer's Hands* (Phillipsburg, NJ: P&R Publishing, 2002), 62.

2. It is becoming increasingly difficult to discipline our children, let alone to make it a teaching event. Even in the church, corporal punishment is under attack. A Christian woman from Massachusetts,

upset at the use of flexible nylon spanking sticks, started a Web site called "Parenting in Jesus' Footsteps." She contends that Jesus would never spank children. Her Web site models either biblical illiteracy or rebellion against God—or both. You can't parent in Jesus' footsteps unless you use corporal punishment. Jesus is the Word of God. That means that every word in the Bible is his. Here is what Jesus commands: "Blows that wound cleanse away evil; strokes make clean the innermost parts" (Prov. 20:30).

It is going to require increasing faith and determination to persist in spanking. Indications are that it might soon be illegal. It is already illegal in Europe, and Canada is becoming increasingly hostile to corporal punishment.

3. Pat Fabrizio, *Under Loving Command* (Cupertino, CA: DIME Publishers, 1969). This booklet had a tremendous impact on Judy and me when our children were young. If read with an attitude of grace, it is highly recommended!

4. *The Works of John Wesley*, vol. 7, sermon no. 95 (Albany, OR: Ages Software, 1997).

Chapter Ten: Food for the Hungry

1. Voddie Baucham Jr., *Family Driven Faith* (Wheaton: Crossway, 2007), 118.

2. George Barna, *Revolutionary Parenting* (Carol Stream, IL: Tyndale, 2007), 30–32.

3. The texts commanding fathers to teach their children are significant: "For I have chosen [Abraham], that he may command his children and his household after him to keep the way of the LORD by doing righteousness and justice, so that the LORD may bring to Abraham what he has promised him" (Gen. 18:19); "Only take care, and keep your soul diligently, lest you forget the things that your eyes have seen, and lest they depart from your heart all the days of your life. Make them known to your children and your children's

children—how on the day that you stood before the LORD your God at Horeb, the LORD said to me, 'Gather the people to me, that I may let them hear my words, so that they may learn to fear me all the days that they live on the earth, and that they may teach their children so'" (Deut. 4:9–10); "You shall therefore lay up these words of mine in your heart and in your soul. . . . You shall teach them to your children, talking of them when you are sitting in your house, and when you are walking by the way, and when you lie down, and when you rise" (Deut. 11:18–19); "He established a testimony in Jacob and appointed a law in Israel, which he commanded our fathers to teach to their children, that the next generation might know them, the children yet unborn, and arise and tell them to their children" (Ps. 78:5–6); "By wisdom a house is built, and by understanding it is established; by knowledge the rooms are filled with all precious and pleasant riches" (Prov. 24:3 4); "Fathers, do not provoke your children to anger, but bring them up in the discipline and instruction of the Lord" (Eph. 6:4).

4. Steve Wright, *reThink* (Wake Forest, NC: InQuest Ministries, 2007), 83.

5. John Flavel, *The Mystery of Providence* (1678; repr., Edinburgh: Banner of Truth, 1995), 57.

6. Jeramy Clark and Jerusha Clark, *After You Drop Them Off* (Colorado Springs: Waterbrook Press, 2005), 192, quoted in Wright, *rethink*, 20.

7. John Piper, *The Pleasures of God* (Sisters, OR: Multnomah, 2000), 289.

8. Douglas Wilson, *Standing on the Promises* (Moscow, ID: Canon Press, 1997), 81.

9. Ibid.

10. Madeline Levine, *The Price of Privilege* (New York: Harper-Collins, 2006), 33.

11. Barna, *Revolutionary Parenting*, 31.

12. Robert M. M'Cheyne, *The Sermons of Robert M. M'Cheyne* (Edinburgh: Banner of Truth, 1961), 29.

Chapter Eleven: Gospel Love

1. Dietrich Bonhoeffer, *Life Together* (New York: Harper and Row, 1954).

2. George Marsden, *Jonathan Edwards: A Life* (New Haven: Yale University Press, 2004), 188–89.

3. John Hannah, *To God Be the Glory* (Wheaton, IL: Crossway, 2000), 16–17.

4. Steve Farrar, *King Me* (Chicago: Moody, 2005).

5. Ibid., 12.

6. Ross Campbell, *How to Really Love Your Child* (Wheaton, IL: Victor, 1985), 80–81. This book is an excellent manual on how to communicate love and affection.

7. James Robison, *In Search of a Father* (Carol Stream, IL: Tyndale, 1979), 55.

8. David Popenoe, *Life without Father* (New York: The Free Press, 1996), 148–49.

9. Ibid., 150.

10. Michael Lamb, ed., *The Role of the Father in Child Development* (New York: Wiley, 1976), 104.

11. Robison, *In Search of a Father*, 174–80.

12. Peter Wyden and Barbara Wyden, *Growing Up Straight* (Lanham, MD: Stein and Day, 1968), 60–61.

13. Lamb, *The Role of the Father in Child Development*, 127.

14. Tedd Tripp, *Shepherding a Child's Heart* (Wapwallopen, PA: Shepherd Press, 1995), xviii.

15. Campbell, *How to Really Love Your Child*; Ross Campbell, *How to Really Love Your Teenager* (Wheaton, IL: Victor, 1985).

16. Robison, *In Search of a Father*. See chapter 5, especially pages 55 to 56.

Chapter Twelve: Amazing Grace

1. Jerry Bridges picked up this well-known slogan from his friend Jack Miller.

2. John Newton, "Amazing Grace," 1779.

Bill Farley worked for many years in the business world while serving the church as a lay pastor. In 1998 he retired from his business to write and to enter full-time ministry. He currently pastors Grace Christian Fellowship in Spokane, Washington, and has written extensively for many Christian publications, including *Discipleship Journal, Focus On The Family Magazine, The Journal of Biblical Counseling, Enrichment Journal,* and *Reformation 21*. His books include *For His Glory* and *Outrageous Mercy*. He has also been a guest writer for his local newspaper, *The Spokesman Review,* and has been featured on a number of radio talk shows.

Bill is the father of five adult children and grandfather of 16 grandchildren. He has been married to his best friend, Judy, for nearly 40 years. His passion is God's glory. He loves to preach it and write about it, especially how it is displayed in our families, local churches, and work environments.

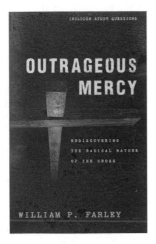

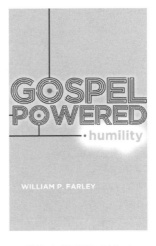

978-1-59638-134-6

978-1-59638-240-4

Outrageous Mercy shows that the cross of Christ is the heart and soul of the Christian life. At the cross we learn everything we need to know about God, man, eternity, wisdom, worship, suffering, and a host of other subjects. Includes study questions for each chapter.

"Farley's argument is bracing and presented with clarity. . . . I found his work stimulating for meditating upon and proclaiming the faith."
—Robert Carroll Walters,
The Living Church

Humility, while essential for conversion and sanctification, is the least emphasized virtue. Farley alerts us to the problem and shows how ours is a humbling gospel, stressing the need for a ministry that promotes humility.

"*Gospel-Powered Humility* carefully grounds humility in the good news of the gospel. This is a book that will teach and convict every believer."
—Tim Challies, blogger, author, and social media consultant

More from P&R Publishing

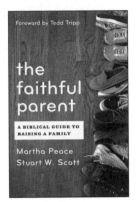

To order, visit www.prpbooks.com
Or call 1(800) 631-0094

Parents and children need help from the One who is perfect, who understands our need, and who can really help us. Martha Peace and Stuart Scott join forces to challenge you to become a faithful parent—one who perseveres and leaves the results to God.

"*The Faithful Parent* provides the comprehensive help that parents need. . . . The authors are seasoned Christians who are safe spiritual guides. . . . This will be a timeless resource for faithful parents."

—TEDD TRIPP

"I wholeheartedly recommend this book. . . . Thank you, Stuart and Martha, for providing a parenting book that is biblical, practical, and specific."

—WAYNE A. MACK

More from P&R Publishing

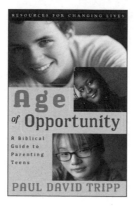

To order, visit www.prpbooks.com
Or call 1(800) 631-0094

Paul Tripp uncovers the heart issues affecting parents and their teenagers during the often chaotic adolescent years. With wit, wisdom, humility, and compassion, he shows parents how to seize the countless opportunities to deepen communication, learn, and grow with their teenagers.

"*Age of Opportunity* is a marvel. It brims with fresh, rich, honest truth. Tripp will get you looking in the mirror before you go looking at your teen. He'll get you seeking—and finding—your own Father's help."

—DAVID POWLISON

"A wealth of biblical wisdom and a treasure of practical steps for understanding and shepherding your teen's heart."

—TEDD TRIPP

More from P&R Publishing

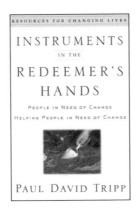

To order, visit www.prpbooks.com
Or call 1 (800) 631-0094

Paul Tripp helps us discover where change is needed in our own lives and the lives of others. Following the example of Jesus, Tripp reveals how to get to know people, and how to lovingly speak truth to them.

"Helps us help others (and ourselves) by giving grace-centered hope that we can indeed change, and by showing us the biblical way to make change happen."

—SKIP RYAN

"Tripp unites a loving heart with a mind trained to the Scriptures. This book is a great companion for pastors and counselors. It will guide anyone who wants to give real help to others, the saving help that is found in Christ's redeeming work."

—RICHARD D. PHILLIPS

More from P&R Publishing

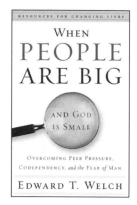

To order, visit www.prpbooks.com
Or call 1(800) 631-0094

"Need people less. Love people more. That's the author's challenge. . . . He's talking about a tendency to hold other people in awe, to be controlled and mastered by them, to depend on them for what God alone can give. . . . [Welch] proposes an antidote: the fear of God."

—*DALLAS MORNING NEWS*

"Biblical and practical. . . . Opens our eyes and directs us back to God and his Word to overcome the fear of man."

—*THE BAPTIST BULLETIN*

"Much needed in our own day. . . . Here is a volume that church libraries and book tables ought to have. Its theme is contemporary. Its answer is thoroughly biblical."

—*THE PRESBYTERIAN WITNESS*